McCOY

edited by
BROUGH SCOTT

RACING POST

This edition first published in Great Britain in 2010 by Racing Post Books
Compton, Newbury, Berkshire, RG20 6NL

10 9 8 7 6 5 4 3 2

A catalogue record for this book is available from the British Library.

ISBN 978-1-905156-80-1

Designed by SoapBox
www.soapboxcommunications.co.uk

Printed in the UK by Butler Tanner and Dennis Ltd, Frome

Every effort has been made to fulfil requirements with regard to copyright material. The publisher will be glad to rectify any omissions at the earliest opportunity.

www.racingpost.com/shop

All the photographs in this book are courtesy the Racing Post, with the following exceptions: Pat Healy (pages 11, 14 and 16), Caroline Norris (pages 12, 18, 20, 21 and 203).

Half title: AP McCoy winning on Refinement at Aintree, April 2006.

Frontispiece: Coming back after winning the 2010 John Smith's Grand National on Don't Push It.

CONTENTS

INTRODUCTION *by Brough Scott*

It happened at Aintree. Many great things have happened there since the weird and wonderful event that has become the Grand National was first run in 1839. But nothing in all that time has matched the moment on 10 April 2010 when Don't Push It gave Tony McCoy his first National at the 15th attempt. The moment when the whole global audience realised quite what a man was in their midst, and when that man finally understood not just what he had done for himself but what he meant to everyone else.

Of course, not one in all those millions of watchers could truly appreciate what it had taken for the angel-faced little boy who first rode in a race in September 1990 to become the hardened superhero who finally scaled the Grand National peak. But they could sense it. And they could see that he got it too.

Suddenly all those years rolled back. The bare statistics – 13,000 rides, 3,000 jumping winners, 15 consecutive championships – are awesome enough and unmatched by anyone in any sport. But they have been achieved on a uniquely demanding and dangerous treadmill where injuries are regular, travel incessant, hunger constant and competitors out to best you every day. Season after season McCoy has clambered up the mountain, setting new records, overcoming agonies, boiling off the pounds, hurling himself and his horses at fences and relentlessly striving to the finishing line. He has never asked for sympathy nor even played easy with the crowds, but up to 2010 he had still never made it to the Grand National summit. And when he did, he realised what a lifetime and life-force had been involved in reaching it.

As the cheers rocked on and the TV and newspaper tributes began to roll, it was clear that it was time to tell his story. But then a sudden dawning came – that at the Racing Post we already had. Every single one of those rides since the first one at Phoenix Park with his father Peadar watching had been logged in our pages. Every result, even the unhappy one that recorded a simple 'F' for fall against his debut *attempt at steeplechasing, every one of those 3,000 winners had been indexed in our results.*

But much, much more than all those scarcely credible facts, our writers and photographers have been with McCoy as the boy became the man became the icon of today. They have recorded the triumphs and disasters, talked to and pictured him in happiness and anger, on the track and off it, in assorted hospital rooms and varied houses – even, on one extremely chilly occasion, in a recuperative 'freeze chamber' with the dial set at -135°C. For twenty years we had been telling the McCoy story in the present tense.

As ideas for a tribute book go it was a 'no-brainer'. That was until we appreciated the scale of the task of compressing two decades of newsprint into just one volume. It has only been achieved because of workers worthy of their subject. Step forward Sean Magee, book creator supreme; John Schwartz, designer of delight; and Julian Brown and James de Wesselow, calling the shots back at base.

But no one can produce lasting work from bad material, and the more we looked back, the more admiration we had for the energy, enthusiasm, professionalism, perception and sheer talent of our writers and photographers as they worked against deadlines to bring us their stories. And whilst listing names would be invidious in such company, exception must be made for the Post's *senior photographer Edward Whitaker – go to the picture on pages 134-5 if you have to ask why.*

However, all of this is for nothing compared with the jewel at the heart of the journey. For while in compiling this book I am very proud of how we have logged it, we can all be prouder still of a man they call Tony McCoy.

BEGINNINGS

FOR a long time Racing Post *readers knew nothing about Tony McCoy. Indeed, it was three full years between the 10-pound claiming apprentice AP McCoy being listed against a horse called Nordic Touch in the six-furlong handicap at the now defunct Dublin racecourse Phoenix Park for his very first ride in public on 1 September 1990 and the actual first mention of his name when riding*

5.00	Olympic Handicap			Gf

14 DECLARED

£4,000 added **For** 3yo + **Minimum Weight** 7-7 **Penalties** after calculation of the handicap win 5lb, value £2,000 or collectively £2,600 7lb; value £2,700 or collectively £3,700 9lb; value £3,400 or collectively £5,100 12lb **Weight-for-age** 3 from 4yo + 3lb **Entries** 44 pay £10 **Acceptors** 19 pay £20 **Penalty Value 1st** £2,770 **2nd** £650 **3rd** £290 **4th** £170

1 323616 **ST AME**26 Ⓒ ....D K Weld 4 10-05 b ..M J Kinane 12
Dr Michael Smurfit —*yellow, royal blue epaulets, royal blue sleeves, yellow seams, yellow cap, royal blue star*

2 770208 **IS KING**49 ⒸⅮ ....C Collins 7 9-10 ....—8
Mrs C Collins —*old rose & pale pink quartered, rose coll. & cuffs, pale pink slvs., qtd. cap.*

3 1-43529 **DICKENS LANE**105 Ⅾ ....M Halford 3 9-09 ....J Reid 9
Mrs M A Walsh —*dark blue, white diamond and hoop on sleeves, quartered cap*

4 141207 **WILD JESTER**7 ⒸⅮ ....Patrick Joseph Flynn 4 9-09 ....J F Egan 13
Mrs E Phelan —*emerald green, white sash, striped cap*

5 066841 **RATHBAWN REALM**21 Ⓒ ....K Prendergast 3 8-12 .....R M Burke (6) 3
Mrs J W Reynolds —*yellow, grey triple diamond, grey sleeves, yellow diamonds, quartered cap*

6 90-0977 **ROESBORO**8 Ⓒ ....J P Kavanagh 4 8-11 ....C Roche 1
Miss S McDonald —*pink, grey stars, quartered cap*

7 208109 **TOWN ABLAZE**49 Ⅾ ....C C Ryan 6 8-06 .....J P Murtagh 10
J D Clague —*maroon, black cross belts, white cap.*

8 4-96775 **ANKA (GER)**8 ....M Kauntze 3 8-04 b..W J O'Connor (2) 4
A Boesso —*dark blue & yellow check, yellow sleeves, dark blue armlet, qtd. cap*

9 884875 **BLUSHING BUNNY**2 ....Peter Casey 4 8-03 b ....W J Smith (6) 2
Mrs Peter Casey —*light blue, red star, red slvs & cap*

10 064446 **NATTY RED**14 ....D Cordell-Lavarack 3 7-11 N G McCullagh (4) 11
Stablemate Racing plc —*black, red diamond and diamond on sleeves, red cap*

11 943647- **HESH-BON**424 ....Peter Casey 6 7-07 ......R Hughes (4) 7
T J Moore —*green, yellow hoop on body & slvs., yellow cap.*

12 556022 **NORDIC TOUCH**4 ⒷⒻ...........J S Bolger 3 7-07 b A P McCoy (10) 5
Mrs J S Bolger —*black, yellow cap, black hoop*

13 68-00 **ON MICHELLES TERM**84 .....Miss C Crothers 3 7-07 ....—14
James Francis Kearns —*black, yellow star and stars on sleeves, black cap, yellow star*

14 00-8700 **ROUNDSTONE LASS**10 ⅮJ C Hayden 4 7-07 b ....—6
E D Gilmartin —*white, maroon chevron, yellow sleeves, white cap, maroon spots*

LAST YEAR: Is King .... 09 04 ....P. Shanahan

BETTING FORECAST: 5-2 St Ame, 4 Is King, 5 Wild Jester, 6 Rathbawn Realm, 15-2 Nordic Touch, 8 Dickens Lane, 10 Anka, Natty Red, 12 Roesboro, Town Ablaze, Blushing Bunny, 16 bar

SPOTLIGHT

IS KING may not be quite the force he was but Con Collins's seven year old will appreciate the cut in the ground and could go close. Without a win since landing this event last year he may account for **Rathbawn Realm**, suited by the slow pace when winning over seven furlongs here last month and who is probably more effective at this trip.

Wild Jester has run his best races at The Park and must also be considered. Never in the hunt behind Spy School over the minimum trip at The Curragh last week Pat Flynn's four year old may rate a greater danger than **Nordic Touch**, runner-up to easy winner Crimson Glen at Tralee, or top weight **St Ame**.

TONY O'HEHIR

Previous spread: Soon to be crowned champion conditional jockey, AP McCoy (black cap) wins the Castle Ashby House Novices' Selling Hurdle at Towcester on Walking Tall, 8 May 1995.

the filly Zavaleta to win the otherwise unsung Autumn Nursery at Leopardstown on 23 October 1993.

Nothing much more was written about him until he moved to England in August 1994, and then the focus tended to be on the winners ridden and those to come. Over the years we picked up all sorts of strands of the story, but it took until the passing of the utterly incredible milestone of 3,000 winners over jumps in February 2009 before one of our writers went back to the very beginning.

You will find that David Ashforth was worth the wait.

IN IRELAND, they call him Anthony; not Tony, nor 'AP'. Those are names people gave him in Britain. At home he was, and still is, Anthony McCoy.

Ireland is a famous school for jockeys, but County Antrim, in Northern Ireland, where McCoy grew up, is not. 'I never thought he'd be a jockey,' says Peadar McCoy, Anthony's father. 'There were no jockeys about here, ever.'

Peadar's family were not involved in racing but after his marriage to Claire, Peadar, a joiner, added three stables to the bungalow he had built in his home village of Moneyglass, and bought a mare called Fire Forest.

AP and his father Peadar McCoy after Colbert Station had won at Leopardstown, 24 January 2010.

Billy and Yvonne Rock with their protégé, November 2002. Billy died the following year.

In 1976, aged two, Anthony sat on Fire Forest's daughter, Misclaire, the dam of Thumbs Up, winner of the 1993 County Hurdle.

That was all Anthony did, for his early passions were soccer and snooker. Later, he joined his elder sisters, Anne-Marie and Roisin, at Miss Kyle's riding school. 'From the first day, Miss Kyle picked him out as having a great seat on a horse,' Peadar remembers. 'That was his first proper ride, and then he wanted a pony.'

The pony Peadar got for him was dedicated to kicking, biting and bucking. Unlike the pony, Peadar was reluctant to bury his son, so exchanged it for a more co-operative version, called Chippy. Chippy quickly amassed a grand collection of gymkhana rosettes but Anthony soon abandoned him for something grander, at Billy Rock's.

Rock, who trained at Cullybackey, about ten miles from the McCoys, was a close friend of Peadar. 'I always used to go to Billy's yard on Saturdays,' says Peadar, 'to watch the horses work. One Saturday, Anthony came with me and, soon after, Billy put him on a horse. After that, I couldn't get him to ride the pony any more.'

Nor go to St Olcan's High School, in nearby Randalstown. The school bus stopped outside their house but the few yards from the front door to the bus door might as well have been the Irish Sea when Claire engaged in the morning ritual of trying to persuade Anthony to make the journey.

'Believe you me, it was a battle,' says Claire, not a weak woman; far from it. 'I forever had the attendance officers at the door because Anthony totally refused to go to school.

'I did get him to a parent-teachers' night once. Mr O'Grady, the headmaster, asked Anthony what he was going to be and Anthony mumbled, "I'm going to be a jockey." "Well," said Mr O'Grady, "you'll need GCSEs if you're going to be a joiner." "I said a jockey," Anthony mumbled again. "Well," said the headmaster, "if Lester Piggott had got his maths GCSE he wouldn't be in prison now for getting his sums wrong on his tax return."'

'Anthony was a lovely, quiet lad,' says O'Grady, now in charge of St Patrick's College, Belfast. 'Not a great attender. He devoted time to his first love, which was horses. Although he didn't take his exams, I believe he had a good education. I'm very proud of him.'

For Anthony, the attractions of maths lessons could not compare with the lessons learned and the money earned with Rock, an accomplice in McCoy's increasing truancy. To make sure that his own attendance plans were not foiled, McCoy paid £100 for a top-of-the-range bicycle, and cycled to Cullybackey.

Rock died in 2003, aged 57, but Yvonne, his wife, remembers McCoy's cycling exploits well. 'I don't know how he did it,' she says. 'The roads were terrible, and so steep we could hardly get up them in a car, but "Wee Anthony", as Billy called him, was mad keen. He'd be the first in the yard in the morning, in the tack room for 6am, before the other lads had thought of getting out of bed.'

The first horse McCoy rode was Wood Louse, chosen for his quietness, but soon Rock was happy to put 'Wee Anthony' up on anything.

'He was only about five foot tall, very small and very shy and quiet,' says Yvonne. 'He would sit at the kitchen table, hardly eat and only speak if you asked him something, but Billy said to me, "This wee lad has great potential. He's a great shape on a horse

> 'He'd be first in the yard in the morning, in the tack room for 6am, before the other lads had thought of getting out of bed.'
>
> YVONNE ROCK

13

'Wee Anthony' and Yvonne Rock lead in Wood Louse, ridden by Conor O'Dwyer, after winning at Downpatrick on 28 July 1989.

and so gutsy." The other lads were 25 or 26 years old and this wee schoolboy rode better than them. Billy thought a lot of him.'

Ian Ferguson, who trains from a nearby yard, was a friend of Rock.

'One day, this young, small kid appeared,' Ferguson recalls, 'and Billy told me he could ride strong horses that older, stronger riders couldn't cope with. He was very proud of Anthony.'

McCoy became part of the team and in 1989, aged 15, he led Wood Louse in after Conor O'Dwyer won on him at Downpatrick. Later that summer, Rock told Peadar that, to get on, Anthony needed to join a bigger yard.

He arranged for McCoy to spend part of his school holiday at Jim Bolger's.

It would soon be the end of McCoy's bicycle rides to Cullybackey, but not the end of the association.

When Anthony McCoy signed up as an apprentice with Jim Bolger, Ian Ferguson, who knew what the unknown rider could do, started to use him.

'He was a very quiet lad but, in his riding, always very positive and confident,' Ferguson remembers.

'Even as an apprentice, he seemed to have races sized up, and knew the opposition, and he was very strong.'

In 1994, aged twenty, McCoy rode a quick double on Ferguson's Huncheon Chance, over hurdles at Down Royal and then on the Flat at Sligo. A month later, he rode Huncheon Chance on the Flat at Bellewstown, in a race in which he claimed 8lb.

'The owners liked a bet and, before Anthony left the paddock, he was made aware of it,' says Ferguson. 'He fought out a finish with Celibate, with John Egan on board, and won by a head. His strength won the race.'

After moving to Britain, McCoy still occasionally rode for Ferguson and Rock. In 1995, and again the following year, he won at Perth on Rock's Tabu Lady. 'We were all there,' Yvonne Rock remembers, 'and Billy was over the moon.'

In November 2002, a few months before Rock succumbed to cancer, they travelled to Britain to see McCoy.

'It was brilliant,' says Yvonne. 'We stayed at Anthony's home and he was able to take Billy to see Jonjo O'Neill's yard and go racing at Newbury. It was a special time.'

That year, McCoy dedicated his autobiography to Billy Rock, 'who treated me like a man when I was a boy and who saw more in the boy than any other man.' Since then, McCoy has regularly paid tribute to his early mentor.

After attending Rock's funeral in April 2003, McCoy flew to Fairyhouse to ride in the Irish Grand National.

'We watched it on television,' says Yvonne. 'It was very sad, yet great. Then, that September, me, my son Timothy and daughter Lynn went to a breeders' awards gala to receive an award Billy had won. Suddenly, Anthony appeared to present it. I had no idea he was there. It made the night.'

Last year, when Lynn got married, McCoy was there with his wife, Chanelle, and the Rock family watched him diligently on television.

'Sometimes,' says Yvonne, 'I can't believe that it's the Wee Anthony that used to sit here, hardly speaking.'

'You couldn't have thought he'd have achieved what he has,' says Ferguson. 'The things he's done are phenomenal.'

McCoy's success has sparked interest in racing where there was little before, in and around Moneyglass, but it has left his family remarkably untouched by his celebrity. His brother, Colm, lives in the bungalow his father built, while Anthony's parents live in the house that Peadar was brought up in, not grand but homely, with Roisin's hairdressing salon next door.

Naturally open and friendly, their son's success has not changed Peadar and Claire. Peadar, quiet, affable and easy going, Claire loud, loquacious and laughing.

'He's very good to us, to every one of us,' says Claire but, as Roisin says, 'I suppose we take it for granted, but we are all very proud of him.'

Last year Kelly, his youngest sister, stayed with Anthony. 'Every evening, from when he came in the door until 10 o'clock at night, he'd watch replays of his races,' she says. 'He'd even watch the ones he'd won to see if he could have ridden a better race. He's still trying to improve.'

That's a champion.

Twenty years ago, Peadar and Claire McCoy drove their 15-year-old son Anthony to Jim Bolger's racing stables. Bolger's yard is hidden away in the lanes and hills on the borders of Carlow and Kilkenny, a very long way from Antrim.

Claire was heartbroken. 'I knew he was going away,' she says, 'but I thought he'd come back. It was in the wilds and Anthony

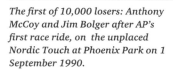

The first of 10,000 losers: Anthony McCoy and Jim Bolger after AP's first race ride, on the unplaced Nordic Touch at Phoenix Park on 1 September 1990.

wasn't 16, but he went back.' In 1990, McCoy signed on for a three-year apprenticeship.

'He looked angelic in those days,' Bolger remembers, 'and was able to ride at 7st 10lb when he started. As far as any young fellow of 16 can tick all the boxes, Anthony did. He had the cut of a jockey about him, was smart and had perfect manners.

'There was a fair bit of competition for rides here but he was certainly up there with Paul Carberry, and easier to teach. There weren't any negatives, he just needed experience. I must have thought a fair bit of him because, when he had his first ride, I made sure he was photographed.'

That was at Phoenix Park on 1 September 1990, when McCoy made his debut on Nordic Touch.

4.00 **Silvermines Maiden** 26/5/92

[OFF 4.03] (1m4f 110y) 1m4½f

For: 3yo only, maidens at starting 1st IR£2,243 2nd IR£520 3rd IR£228 4th IR£130

1	LEGAL STEPS (IRE) (15) 3 8-01 .... A P McCoy (10)	
	gr f by Law Society (USA)—Keep In Step (Dance In	
	Time)	20/1
2	8 ANTHIS (IRE) (4) 3 8-11 .... W J O'Connor	
	b f by Ela-Mana-Mou—Rosolini (Ragusa)	4/1C
3	1½ SAKANDA (IRE) (17) 3 8-11 .... R Hughes	
	b f by Vayrann—Sellasia (FR) (H.H.AgaKhan)	8/1
4	½ LET IT RIDE (IRE) (8) 3 9-00 .... N G McCullagh	4/1C
5	3 NORTHMAID (IRE) (14) 3 8-11 .... C Roche	4/1C
6	PLUMBOB (IRE) (10) 3 9-00 .... E A Leonard	16/1
7	AEGEAN FANFARE (IRE) (3) 3 8-04 .... P P Murphy	
		(10) 14/1
8	PENNINE GIRL (IRE) (2) 3 8-07 ..... R M Burke (4)	20/1
9	ANNA DEAR (IRE) (9) 3 8-05 .... M Fenton (6)	33/1
10	TANAISTE (USA) (12) 3 9-00 .... S Craine	8/1
11	HAWAIAN TASCA (IRE) (11) 3 8-08 .... D G O'Shea	
		(6) 14/1
12	VICOSA (IRE) (7) 3 9-00 .... K J Manning	20/1
13	MAGICAL HEIGHTS (IRE) (16) 3 8-11 ..... P V Gilson	8/1
14	LAW FACULTY (IRE) (13) 3 9-00b'...... M J Kinane	11/2
15	WANDERING THOUGHTS (IRE) (1) 3 8-08 T J O'Sullivan	
		(6) 33/1
16	VICTORY TOAST (IRE) (6) 3 8-11 .... W J Supple	12/1
17	PEACE CARRIER (IRE) (5) 3 8-11 .... J C Barker	12/1

17 ran   TIME: 2m 56.3s   SP TOTAL PERCENT 163

1st OWNER: MrE.P.Spillane TRAINER: J.S.Bolger (Coolcullen, Co. Carlow) BRED: BarronstownBloodstockLtd
2nd OWNER: MajorVictorMcCalmont TRAINER: M.Kauntze
3rd OWNER: MrDavidBrennan TRAINER: PatrickMullins
TOTE: WIN £122.80 PL £24.80,£2.20,£7.80 DF: £259.70

There was no sudden stardom. Bolger believed in the value of learning. 'Pat Eddery had 70 rides before his first winner,' he observes, 'but, from the start, McCoy was a very confident and safe rider. He never succeeded in getting a horse kicked on the gallops and, along with Carberry and Paddy Brennan, he didn't get bucked off easily.'

Bolger's confidence was reflected in McCoy's appearances riding work on the backs of Jet Ski Lady, the 1991 Oaks winner, and St Jovite, who won the 1992 Irish Derby and King George VI and Queen Elizabeth Diamond Stakes.

On 26 March 1992, McCoy rode his first winner, on Legal Steps, at Thurles. He was still only 17. The following January, he broke his left leg badly when Kly Green unseated him on the gallops.

When he returned, several months later, he was taller and heavier, his future clearly as a jump jockey.

McCoy had his first success over hurdles at Gowran Park on 20 April 1994 on Riszard, a horse that Mr AP O'Brien, the stable's amateur rider and future champion trainer, had ridden to victory in a bumper race the previous year.

First of many: Legal Steps, ridden by AP McCoy, winning the Silvermines Maiden at Thurles, 26 March 1992.

'Anthony was tall, very slight and thin, and an unbelievable rider for his age,' Aiden O'Brien remembers. 'It was the way he sat and the balance he had.

'He was very quiet and mannerly. For a young fellow, he was unbelievably dedicated and committed and very focused. He had a lot of wisdom for his age.'

McCoy impressed everyone at the yard. 'He was always very stylish and very determined,' says Seamie Heffernan, another member of Bolger's talented team. 'He was a very natural rider and a straightforward person.'

'Anthony was a natural rider and horseman,' says Ted Durcan, 'with lovely hands and amazing balance and very brave. He made everything look easy.'

McCoy gradually became more familiar with the winner's enclosure, and ambitious for success. 'He was always a very straightforward fellow,' says Bolger. 'What you saw was what you got. The only thing hidden from me was his ambition. I probably saw only 25 per cent of that. By then, he was very marketable, and he was poached twelve months earlier than I'd have liked.'

On 15 July 1994 McCoy, aged 20 and still claiming 7lb, won a hurdle race on Mollie Wootton at Kilbeggan.

It was his last winning ride before moving to England. Four days later, Toby Balding, alerted to McCoy's talent, met him at Wexford and offered him a job. When McCoy accepted, he had ridden in just over 100 races, won six on the Flat and seven over hurdles, and had yet to ride in a chase. When he did, on No Sir Rom at Galway on July 30, he fell.

'I wanted him to stay for another year,' says Bolger. 'He had broken his leg in a very soft fall and I was very concerned about that. We were getting him going and, if he had waited twelve months he'd have ridden a lot of winners in Ireland and we would have looked after him.

'As it turned out, he didn't have the bad fall I feared, but that doesn't mean my view was wrong. Now, my staff and I are Anthony's biggest fans, and he knows that.'

Everyone has the same reaction the day after a member of the family has ridden their first winner – rush to the paper shop to see what the Racing Post *has said about it. On 27 March 1992, the day after their son Anthony had steered a horse called Legal Steps smoothly clear of 16 rivals at Thurles, the McCoys were to be disappointed. Well down the dispatch the horse was mentioned, and the trainer – but nothing about the jockey.*

JIM BOLGER'S excellent start to the new Flat campaign continued with Legal Steps (Silvermines Maiden) and Nordic Gayle (Galtee Handicap) completing a double bringing the Coolcullen trainer's total to seven.

Times would change.

As David Ashforth explained above, whatever hopes young McCoy had of staying at Flat racing weights were dashed when he snapped his left leg almost in half one cold morning in Coolcullen in January 1993. When he got home from hospital he weighed 7st 7lb. When he finally returned to Bolger's he was 9st 2lb, and when he got back on

The comeback: AP and Zavaleta winning the Autumn Nursery at Leopardstown, 23 October 1993.

the racecourse on a horse with the inviting name of Bubbly Prospect at Gowran Park in August 1993, he was not that comfortable at 8st 6lb.

But come the end of October, 18 months after that first winner on Legal Steps, the second came. It was at Leopardstown on a two-year-old filly called Zavaleta, and this time there was a mention in Tony O'Hehir's report.

APPRENTICE Anthony McCoy, out of action for most of the season after breaking a leg in a fall on Jim Bolger's gallops in the spring, rode his second winner when guiding Zavaleta to a cosy two-length win from Sophie's Pet in the Autumn Nursery.

Yet this was hardly a full-page feature, and when McCoy first had his name in the jumps results it was for being brought down at the last hurdle on a Bolger runner called Riszard at Leopardstown in March 1994. But a month later he won on the same horse at Gowran Park, and if he wasn't being written about in the Racing Post, *at least he was making an impression on people that mattered.*

AP McCOY'S RECORD IN IRELAND BEFORE MOVING TO ENGLAND IN 1994

IRISH FLAT

	wins	runs	total prize money in £
1990	0	2	466
1991	0	17	1,424
1992	1	23	5,196
1993	1	11	3,640
1994	4	16	12,606

IRISH JUMPS

	wins	runs	total prize money in £
1994-95	4	24	16,258

AP wins the Drumree Handicap at Navan on Gallardini, 14 May 1994.

21

Most crucially, in this instance, on trainer Toby Balding, who three years earlier had brought Adrian Maguire back from Ireland to become a young star in the UK.

When McCoy passed Peter Scudamore's jump racing record of 222 winners in a season in March 1998, the trainer told Neil Morrice how it had all started.

TOBY BALDING yesterday reflected on the moment when he decided to employ Tony McCoy as a conditional jockey four years ago.

Balding recalled: 'I was looking for a conditional to take over from Adrian [Maguire] and my man in the north of Ireland, James McNicol, said I should interest myself in this aspirant.

'I saw him ride, was impressed immediately and offered him a summer with us to see how we worked together with regard to him having an ongoing career at Fyfield. It was the very next year after Adrian moved on.'

Balding, keen to sell his protégé to fellow trainers, felt the next important step was to secure him a good agent.

He added: 'The important thing was that in the first instance I was able to sell him and what I saw in him to Dave Roberts, who then put him in with the other people he rode for.

'I think the keynote to his success was his natural ability allied to tremendous dedication.'

It was on 6 August 1994 that the still unknown AP McCoy drove off to the Rosslare ferry, and on the 13th that an otherwise unsung horse called Arctic Life provided his first ride in Britain when running a distant second in the 2m6f Clifford Chambers Novice Hurdle at Stratford-upon-Avon.

Unlike in Ireland, the winners did not have long to wait. At Exeter on 7 September 1994, for the first of what was to prove countless times, Andrew King put McCoy's name into a Racing Post *report.*

MICK FITZGERALD'S bad luck – he's out with an injured wrist – proved to be young Irishman Tony McCoy's good fortune as he rode Chickabiddy to land the concluding handicap hurdle.

After Legal Steps there had been 18 months before the next winner, but now in England it was a bubbling stream – maybe that comeback ride at Gowran Park on Bubbly Prospect had not been so badly named after all.

Will O'Hanlon filed this report from Cheltenham on 29 September 1994.

TOBY BALDING'S promising young rider Tony McCoy, who saw his claim cut to 5lb at Worcester last Saturday, was again seen to good effect as he coaxed Wings Of Freedom home a neck winner of the Frenchie Nicholson Conditional Jockeys Handicap Hurdle from Borrowed And Blue.

McCoy, a 20-year-old from County Antrim, was on cloud nine after his win, saying: 'It's always been a dream of mine to ride a winner at Cheltenham and now I've done it on my very first ride here.' It is unlikely to be his last, especially with the dynamic Dave Roberts plotting his career moves.

Winners change everything. On 30 September, McCoy was a 'promising young rider'. A week later in Andrew King's report from Newton Abbot he was a 'rising star'.

RISING STAR Anthony (AP) McCoy had an afternoon of ups and downs. He was on the deck after Southampton took a last-flight tumble with the St Austell Brewery Claiming Hurdle at his mercy, but bounced back to partner a double via Bonus Boy in the Conditional Jockeys' Selling Handicap Chase and Ask The Governor, who took the handicap hurdle.

The winners kept coming, and experience too. A first ride at the Cheltenham Festival and, on the Martin Pipe-trained Chatam, a first attempt at the Grand National – only to come down at the twelfth fence.

AP, or Tony – as everyone bar his friends and family now called him – was on his way, but was still only categorised in the 'youth team' section.

That was why you had to spin three quarters of the way through Nick Godfrey's magisterial review of the 1994-95 jumping season to read this summary of a first season's effort.

ADRIAN MAGUIRE seems hardly old enough for us to be looking out for the new Adrian Maguire but we found him in conditional champion Tony McCoy whose final tally of 74 broke Maguire's own record for a conditional rider.

If anyone doubted whether the tyro would 'hack it' against his seniors, the next season's statistics soon gave reassurance.

By November 1995 it was high time we took a real long look at him, and for a first and highly revealing time, our Lambourn man Rodney Masters sat down to paint the picture.

IT SOUNDS a mite perverse and excessive but it's impossible to fault its accuracy. Championship pacesetter Tony McCoy declares that breaking his left leg as a teenager was the luckiest break of them all. He was grounded for five and a half months after a gallops accident with a Jim Bolger two-year-old, and inactivity made his gangling pipe-cleaner frame stockpile fat.

He ballooned from 7st 9lb to 9st 7lb, and a career decision he had dithered over was decided for him, with the alternative automatically expunged by the extra baggage.

When carted off by ambulance to hospital he was a Flat jockey. When next seen on a racecourse he was a jump jockey's weight. What happened next continues to leave him in head-spinning disbelief.

In the 15 months since arriving in England, virtually unknown, he has stacked up 130-plus winners; he is currently forcing a hell-for-leather clip in the championship; and he is being extolled as another Maguire.

The 21-year-old non-drinking, non-smoking son of a County Antrim joiner and horse breeder – father Peadar bred Nicky Henderson's County Hurdle winner Thumbs Up – has been leaping three stairs at a time. Self-effacement rather than egotism has been his partner on the journey.

'If anyone had forecast when I arrived in England that I was going to ride 50 winners by the first week of October in only my

McCOY'S SEASON 1994-1995	
wins:	74
rides:	469
strike rate:	16%
position in championship:	7th

behind:
Richard Dunwoody
Adrian Maguire
Norman Williamson
Jamie Osborne
Peter Niven
David Bridgwater

Opposite: AP and What's In Orbit in the United House Construction Chase at Ascot, 28 October 1995. They finished unplaced.

25

A fresh-faced AP in February 1996.

second season, I could have done nothing to stop myself bursting out laughing. The thought alone bordered on madness.

'People are saying I ride like Adrian. But in truth it isn't so. I wouldn't insult anyone by suggesting I ride like them.

'Success has taken me by surprise. I wouldn't be anywhere near as well known as your top jocks, and if people have become more aware as to who I am in recent months, I can't say I've noticed it one bit. I don't think they're talking about me, but if they want to I don't mind. I'm not afraid of the limelight. I can cope with it.'

During his brief career over jumps – his first chasing winner was just over 12 months ago – he has walked away from falls with only a bang and a bruise. The fact that he has been free from a serious bone-cruncher is easy to identify in his no-fear enthusiasm. 'I never worry about the dangers of the sport simply because I don't reckon there are any dangers.

'I love the thrill of riding winners, and I think about little else. The only thing I don't like about being a jockey is getting beat. If I've had a bad day at the races I definitely get down, and have a sulk.'

He says he is quite serious and down to earth. During four years with Bolger he lived with noted fun-lover Paul 'Alice' Carberry, and remembers there was never a dull day. He is searching for a girlfriend – 'but she must be an only child with a father who farms at least 1,000 acres.'

His association with Toby Balding was born from a distant mutual admiration, tied together with the assistance of an expert go-between in Highland Wedding's jockey Eddie Harty, plus additional input from agent Dave Roberts.

Balding was tipped the wink over the young talent from a horse scout contact in Northern Ireland, and McCoy had the Weyhill trainer top of his list because he knew there would be a void with Maguire moving on to David Nicholson. They were introduced by Harty outside the Wexford weighing room.

While with Bolger he had ridden work on some of the best-known horses in Ireland at the time, including Jet Ski Lady, St Jovite and, in particular, Eva Luna.

To no surprise, Bolger – 'Hard but fair, and there can be few better at teaching the game; he insisted we studied the styles of Dettori, Kinane, Dunwoody and Osborne' – was not best pleased when his protégé handed in his notice.

'He was a bit angry to start with, and I could understand his disappointment because he had put a good deal of effort into teaching me the ropes, and here I was off to England after riding only 13 winners (six of them on the Flat). He was anxious to keep me for as long as possible.

'Fortunately, Mr Bolger was all right about it in the end, and I would like to ride for him again during my trips to Ireland.'

Back in County Antrim he has four sisters and a brother, a 15-year-old all-Ireland boxing champion. Although this was McCoy's first visit to England, at no stage was he overcome by pangs of homesickness.

'Some people insisted I was being silly going to Mr Balding because the previous season hadn't been a particularly good one for him, but I didn't view it that way. Every trainer has a bad year here and there, and after all he was without a stable jockey for the coming season.'

In parity with modern fashion, McCoy has no formal retainer, merely an agreement with Balding and Paul Nicholls, and if there is a clash of interests generally the best prospect of a winner will be the overruling factor.

Showing maturity and acumen beyond his years, he is blessed with the diplomacy and side-stepping finesse of a politician when faced with a contentious question.

He ponders long and hard before releasing an answer, aware one word out of place could be misinterpreted. He regularly repeats the same phrase, 'Now we must be careful how we word this.'

During the summer his name was linked with the Martin Pipe vacancy, almost to a point where some assumed he was favourite.

'My name was obviously in the frame because I had a few rides for the stable and was lucky enough to have some winners. I thought I had a chance of getting it, and although in the end I didn't, I was flattered to be shortlisted.'

McCOY'S SEASON 1995-1996	
wins:	175
rides:	759
strike rate:	23%
position in championship:	1st

As they lead the championship charge, there's no animosity with David Bridgwater, who got the Martin Pipe job: 'You couldn't find an easier-going guy.'

McCoy says that, although his main rival is ideally positioned and must be favourite, he terms his own championship odds of 9-2 as realistic.

He emphasises the role of Roberts. 'He enjoys being an agent as much as I enjoy being a jockey. He has played an enormous part in my success and there's no way I could have reached this point without his support.

'Mr Balding has put me straight a few times but he has never given me a proper roasting. I think at the moment he knows I understand how he wants his horses ridden, while perhaps on occasions before I didn't. He reckons I should know what to do without him having to tell me.'

Sons of Ulster figure more prominently than ever before in the championships of both codes with John Reid, Ray Cochrane, Richard Dunwoody, Tony Dobbin and now McCoy regularly making the headlines.

Teachers must be narrating bewitching racing stories in the province's kindergartens. As countryman Frank Carson says, 'It's the way they tell 'em.'

We had much more to learn, but the more we looked, the more relentless the progress. There was, with Kibreet in the Grand Annual, a first winner at the Cheltenham Festival, and at Aintree, with Viking Flagship in the Melling Chase, a big-race victory that really caught the eye.

For a long time in the 1996 Grand National, Deep Bramble was threatening to make this first championship season a sensational one, only to break a bone on the flat two fences from home.

It had been a terrific start, even if Janet Hickman's end-of-season review, having then to be written in Derby week, still had something of a cursory nature about it.

MADE ALL, clear halfway, unchallenged. Tony McCoy failed narrowly to record the fastest 50 and 100, and had the jockeys' title

won by Cheltenham bar injury. He ended with 175 wins, 43 more than nearest pursuer David Bridgwater.

A championship eventually for McCoy, leading conditional in 1994-95 with a record 74 wins in his first British season, was easy to forecast. That it came this term, making him the youngest champion since Josh Gifford in 1962-63, was less predictable. Operating as a freelance, he had a tall task against Martin Pipe's No.1 David Bridgwater and David Nicholson's jockey Adrian Maguire, despite champion Richard Dunwoody's decision to ease off slightly.

But whereas McCoy capitalised on summer jumping, Maguire was sidelined with a broken arm and Pipe moved into gear more sluggishly than usual. Thereafter, thanks to powerful support from Paul Nicholls and Toby Balding and a relatively injury-free run, McCoy never weakened.

There was a very real sense that McCoy was on his way. But, to misquote the words of the song, it was clearly a case of 'We ain't seen nothin' yet.'

RECORD
BREAKER

McCoy was a man on a mission. He wanted to ride everything and attacked every fence as if it was his last. It made punters cheer and old pros quail. 'He'll kill himself,' we used to mutter.

On Boxing Day 1996 he survived a real 'mother and father' of a fall from Mr Mulligan in the King George VI Chase, but in one terrible week in January both the ground and the politics of racing came up to bite him.

Up till then AP had been making hay on runners trained by Paul Nicholls at Ditcheat as well as riding many winners for Martin Pipe. It was not a balancing act that could last.

TONY McCOY will no longer have first choice of Paul Nicholls's horses after falling out with the trainer over riding arrangements at Newton Abbot today.

The shock news was announced by Nicholls yesterday after McCoy had told the trainer that he would not ride Flaked Oats in the Bet With The Tote Novices' Chase, as he intended to partner Martin Pipe's exciting chasing debutant Cyborgo in the same race.

'I'm surprised and disappointed in Tony and I'm just not going to be messed about any more,' Nicholls said yesterday. 'I'm fairly flexible, but Tony and I have a gentleman's agreement that he will ride my horses and he has broken that.

'My owners are giving me grief and I'm afraid Tony will no longer have first choice on my horses. From now on that will go to Philip Hide, and that includes the likes of Belmont King, See More Business, Castlekellyleader, Storm Damage and Cherrynut.'

Nicholls added: 'When Philip is not available I will just use the best available – and that will include Tony if he wants to ride for me, because he's a very good jockey.'

The news is sure to spark speculation that McCoy will link up with Pipe, who lost his stable jockey earlier this season when David Bridgwater deserted his yard.

The six-times champion trainer was playing his cards close to his chest yesterday, but has made no secret about the high regard

Previous spread: AP and See More Business (right) alongside Richard Dunwoody and Dorans Pride at the last fence in the Chiquita Drinmore Novice Chase at Fairyhouse, 1 December 1996. Dorans Pride won by a length.

Pertemps King George VI Chase at Kempton Park, 26 December 1996: Mr Mulligan and AP crash-land as Richard Dunwoody and One Man go on to win.

in which he holds McCoy, who rode the master of Pond House's Make A Stand to victory in the Lanzarote Hurdle at Kempton on Saturday.

Pipe said yesterday: 'The first I heard of any trouble between Paul Nicholls and Tony was when you phoned me. I haven't asked him to be our stable jockey – but it would be interesting, wouldn't it?'

Elaborating on the reasons behind the split, Nicholls continued: 'Basically last night and first thing this morning Tony said he would be on Flaked Oats. At that stage I didn't think Cyborgo would run, but then Pipe changed his mind and Tony said he was getting off mine.

'I told Tony that if he did, he wouldn't ride any of the others tomorrow, but he still decided to ride Cyborgo.

'I explained to Tony that he rides for my yard and that Cyborgo would be coming up against See More Business in the future. Tony said that he would ride See More Business if that happened, but that's no good to me. I need to be able to rely on someone and so do my owners.

'I expected Tony to stick to his word, and he hasn't.'

PAUL NICHOLLS

'I expected Tony to stick to his word, and he hasn't.'

McCoy, who schooled Cyborgo yesterday morning, has ridden 27 winners for Nicholls this season – including Belmont King in the Rehearsal Chase at Chepstow – but Pipe has been his main source of success, providing 35 of his total 125 wins.

The jockey was unavailable for comment about his split with Nicholls, but Hide, attached primarily to Josh Gifford's yard, was understandably delighted to hear the news.

'Obviously we'll have to see what happens over the next few days but yes, I'm delighted by the news,' Hide said.

Bruce Jackson reflected on the break-up.

TONY McCOY'S split with trainer Paul Nicholls yesterday is the first major setback for the rising star of jump racing.

During McCoy's meteoric rise from champion conditional to champion jockey in consecutive seasons, there has been nothing but praise for the young jockey and Nicholls was one of the cheerleaders.

Nicholls, making a name for himself in his own right as a trainer, has been a major contributor to McCoy's cause, providing him with 69 wins from 246 rides for the stable.

Statistics show Nicholls, a former top jockey with trainer David Barons, has been a linchpin in the young jockey's armoury, being the trainer who provided him with most successes in his championship-winning 175.

Equally McCoy helped the Shepton Mallet trainer reach a first 50 in a season, riding 42 of the stable's 53 winners last season.

It had seemed to be a two-way admiration society, which continued to work well this season with Nicholls providing 27 of McCoy's 125 wins so far, second only to Martin Pipe in the supply of the jockey's winners.

Last season McCoy, expressing his appreciation of Nicholls, said: 'The arrangement I have riding for Toby [Balding] and Paul has worked very well and they are happy for me to go where my best chances are. Both of them have been a big help and I take their advice if they think a horse has a really good chance, because they are both very good judges.'

This season had also brought bigger success for the Nicholls–McCoy combine with General Crack winning the Charisma Gold Cup at Kempton and two five-figure hauls at Chepstow courtesy of Gold Cup hope See More Business in the Rising Stars Novices' Chase and Belmont King in the Rehearsal Chase.

These successes started to put the partnership under strain, because until then Nicholls had not had leading performers, which McCoy was being booked for elsewhere by agent Dave Roberts.

This season McCoy has been linked with a number of top rides. His King George ride on Mr Mulligan, despite their last-fence fall, brought a reported promise he would partner last season's leading novice in the Gold Cup.

McCoy's keenness to be associated with top horses has led to more conflicts of interest (he wanted to ride the hurdler Teinein at Sandown on the day he won at Chepstow on Belmont King) and yesterday's latest incident proved one too many for Nicholls.

But if McCoy had to go through a degree of mental anguish over the Cyborgo affair, it was as nothing to the physical smack he would get in Somerset four days later.

TONY McCOY was discharged from hospital last night after a heavy fall at Wincanton – with doubts hanging over his chances of riding at the Cheltenham Festival.

It was initially feared that the champion jockey could be out of action for several months after a crashing fall from Speedy Snapsgem at the first fence in the Maurice Lister Maiden Chase.

McCoy lay prostrate on the ground and was given oxygen by paramedics before being stretchered to the course medical room.

But it later emerged that the injury was not as serious as first thought, although McCoy will still face a battle to regain full fitness before the Festival, which starts on 11 March.

Stretchered off after falling from Speedy Snapsgem at Wincanton, 23 January 1997.

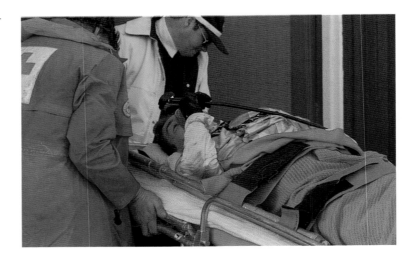

McCoy, 66 clear of Adrian Maguire in this season's jockeys' championship, suffered two fractured bones in his left shoulder in the fall.

He was taken to Yeovil District Hospital for X-rays and driven home later in the evening by his fellow jockey Richard Hughes and Sylvester Kirk, Richard Hannon's assistant. McCoy, heavily sedated, made no comment as he left.

A hospital spokeswoman said: 'We expect him to be out for a few weeks. Whether that is four or six weeks we cannot tell at the moment. It all depends on how the healing process goes. Some people heal more quickly than others.' Trainer Martin Pipe, with whom McCoy strengthened his links this week following his break-up with Paul Nicholls, also arrived at the hospital to monitor the situation.

After leaving the jockey's bedside, Pipe said: 'Tony has broken his scapula – one of the bones is on the top of his shoulder and the other underneath it.

'It is incredible that it isn't worse but it will still be a long time before he can ride again; I think we are looking at about six weeks. He will go home tonight with his left side all strapped up and will have to see a specialist tomorrow.'

Earlier in the week McCoy had split with trainer Nicholls and ironically his horse, Jac del Prince, completed the race safely.

Nicholls said: 'I feel really gutted for Tony. I am genuinely upset for him and the sooner he is back the better from everyone's point of view. It's a bad end to a bad week.'

Little had gone wrong for McCoy this season, until the events of this week.

In November, he shattered by 30 days the record for the fastest 100 previously held by Peter Scudamore. With 130 winners this term, he was on target to lower Scudamore's record of 221 wins in a season.

But even his injury yesterday did not divert his mind from the job for long. 'Have I missed any winners?', he asked Martin Pipe. 'No, you were second,' said the trainer with reference to the effort of D'Naan, whom McCoy would have ridden in the claiming hurdle.

Pipe, who has been using McCoy on a regular basis this term, has booked Richard Dunwoody to ride Pridwell in the Cleeve Hurdle at Cheltenham tomorrow and Or Royal in the 50 Years of Timeform Novices' Handicap Chase. He is already booked for Challenger du Luc in the Ladbroke Trophy.

The young champion was shaken all right – but this was a test of his steel. A month later Rodney Masters went along to see how well he was passing it.

TONY McCOY remembers how on the last occasion we sat around a pub table with a tape recorder between us, 15 months and 243 winners ago, he had been adamant that the worst part of his job was coping with defeat.

'You can amend that quote now,' he laughs, clutching his left shoulder with a mock grimace. 'Now I know the worst part of the job is getting injured.'

He traces an index finger across his scarlet cardigan, from his damaged shoulder to his right shoulder, then down near to the bottom of his ribcage and back to where he began. The area within the triangle had been bruised to a hue more black than blue.

'Though I fractured my left shoulder and collarbone, it was my chest that took the full impact of the fall. There was some internal bleeding and I've been told that I came close to puncturing a lung. I found it difficult to breathe for a while: the pain was desperate, worse than when I broke my leg as a kid.'

As he mended, an amalgam of impatience, frustration and boredom took root because, he says, all he needs out of life right now is winners.

During this enforced time out he refused to log how many have slipped by, but it is impossible to overlook that within one hour at Newbury he missed both Make A Stand and Cyborgo.

Recognising her customer as the champion jockey, Joan the barmaid kindly flashes the Racing Channel to the television in the corner of the pub, and McCoy cannot resist the odd snatched glance.

As a Martin Pipe odds-on shot he would have ridden paddles a fence and forfeits three lengths, he shakes his head. 'He won't get back from there.' He didn't.

McCoy's cushion of a lead in the championship is more of a king-sized mattress, and though there is no threat of surrendering his title, he has been anxious to hurry back, for no other reason than that he is missing it desperately.

In the 30 months since he arrived in Britain he has ridden close on 400 winners with never more than the odd day off due to injury.

Ian Balding approaches our table to wish him a speedy recovery, and thoughtfully inquires as to which shoulder he damaged before shaking his hand. John Francome, champion two names before McCoy's, arrives in the car park in another freshly unwrapped flashy sports car.

'If I end up with a lifestyle anywhere near John's, I'll be happy enough,' admires McCoy. 'He is the one person if you could follow you'd be guaranteed to be doing well.'

Like Francome he neither drinks nor smokes, but as he proved at the well-lubricated shindig after the BBC Sports Personality of the Year awards in December, he is more than content to sit up most of the night partying with people who do.

While others sank pints he sipped Diet Coke throughout, said his farewells at 5.30am and travelled on to Newton Abbot where he rode three winners. He was justifiably peeved when hearing on the radio driving home that he had 'done particularly well because he must have been nursing a hangover.'

Some may worry that the unpretentious McCoy is not fully wringing out the deserved kudos and fun that he might from his treasured, hard-won status as champion. However, this trait is not dissimilar to the most recent of jumping's title holders, and maybe it is a required element of their success.

Most nights he will stay in watching television – live football is a must, particularly his beloved Arsenal – or playing video from his library of racing tapes.

He says: 'In all honesty, I don't actually think of myself in terms of being the champion jockey. Some day, someone is going to take the title, and I believe it will be less of a letdown for me then if I don't get carried away now.

'Anyway it would be silly to get high and mighty over being leading jockey. It hasn't changed my performance one jot. I've all the same friends I had before. I suppose the main advantage of being champion is that it allows me to get on better horses. The other difference I've noticed is that I get recognised a bit more when I go home to County Antrim, though my family treat me no different.'

He says leading the championship tends to induce more than the occasional look behind to identify the youngsters on their way up and most likely to topple him. The faces he sees most often belong to Richard Johnson, Gerry Hogan and Barry Fenton.

But they still have to go some to catch him.

So to Cheltenham 1997 and to Make A Stand and Mr Mulligan, two of the most spectacular rides in the history of the Champion Hurdle and Gold Cup history.

The front running Make A Stand put in, quite simply, the fastest set of hurdle jumping that any of us had ever seen, but Mr Mulligan was something else. Our last sighting of the huge, gangly chesnut had been

> 'Some day, someone is going to take the title, and I believe it will be less of a letdown for me then if I don't get carried away now.'

TONY McCOY

39

of him and McCoy doing a terrifying looking final-fence somersault in the King George at Kempton. If anyone thought that would give his jockey the cue for caution, they had got the wrong man.

God help me, I have seen top jockeys at Cheltenham since the 1950s – but this was almost another dimension, as I wrote at the end of the Festival.

TALENT is not enough. Other jockeys may have had the balance and timing and horsemanship of AP McCoy, certainly some have been neater. But rarely if ever have we had anyone with compulsion to match. This is a driven man. Mr Mulligan, like Make A Stand, knew what it's like to be a driven horse.

It still seems scarcely credible that it is only two and a half years since a then 20-year-old Anthony Peter McCoy rode his first winner in Britain, only five since he rode his first winner of all.

Make A Stand powers up the Cheltenham hill to win the 1997 Smurfit Champion Hurdle from Theatreworld (right) and Space Trucker.

His rise to the top has been such a rocket surge phenomenon that there was a tendency to imagine the heights could never be sustained.

How could you follow an opening season of 74 winners as champion conditional with 174 as champion jockey and then continue upwards?

But he has, oh yes he has, and in the last three days the whole world has had to serve witness.

The tiny five-stoner from the post office in Moneyglass, County Antrim, who used to cycle the twelve miles to Billy Rock's point-to-point yard in Cullybackey, near Ballymena, has grown into a long lean athlete so honed down that his pale skin scarcely seems capable of sweating.

The young apprentice whom Jim Bolger reported as 'not yet a star in the saddle but a star in attitude' has matured into the elite in the first without losing even a degree in the second. Many find themselves broadened but slightly blunted by success, so far McCoy has only been sharpened by it.

That's never been more evident than in his reaction to his broken shoulder seven weeks ago. This was a serious injury, the most serious he has suffered since a bad leg break at Jim Bolger's saw him return six inches taller with any ideas of Flat racing now on short horizons.

It was a fall which most of us thought would rule Cheltenham out of any ordinary calculations. But he was back after a month, albeit looking even more white faced than usual. Did he take it easy? He has ridden every day since, had several hospital-shaped falls and had even Richard Dunwoody suggesting a pre-Festival siesta.

But the key to McCoy is that while he may be obsessive he is anything but moronic. This is no head down, eyes shut, horse flogger. This is a winner prepared to search every angle as well as stretch every sinew for victory, and the joy for history watchers at Cheltenham was that twice in three days he found a horse to match his commitment.

AP may have been in the driving seat, but what a ride he got from Mr Mulligan.

For this giant chesnut is such a long-backed washy-coloured-looking camel that it doesn't take much imagining to see him tripping up on the flat as he did when set to win his first point-to-point in Ireland.

When first at Kim Bailey's, lads hated riding him for fear of stumbling, and his major claim to fame was a notorious, unprompted, neck-breaking somersault two strides after a fence at Newbury.

Noel Chance and Mary Bromiley have done miracles to get the beast to Cheltenham in such mint condition. In a state for McCoy to destroy the dreams of so many.

For this was a round of the most ruthless protection. With a horse as long-striding as Mr Mulligan it is not enough to just kick in and hope. Hand and heel and eye have to be tuned to the roll of the athlete beneath you.

Again and again the big chestnut came up right in the rhythm of his gallop. Down the hill he had Barton Bank embattled beside him, Dorans Pride and especially One Man close up and threatening. This was where the long lanky leader would surely empty.

But he didn't. Oh no he didn't. Much to his own enormous credit but much also to the implacable compulsion of the man on top.

The 1997 Tote Cheltenham Gold Cup. Below: The white-faced Mr Mulligan jumps the first fence between Barton Bank (left) and Dublin Flyer. Opposite: Jubilation in the winner's enclosure.

Many jockeys under ultimate pressure get loose and flappy, McCoy only clamps in tighter still.

It takes terrific strength to apply such short-leathered leg-thrusting. Watch the video, see the message of mind and muscle. It is a signal that we now have a champion to match any that have gone before.

That season ended with 190 winners including the Scottish National on Belmont King, who probably only won it because he (and therefore McCoy) were withdrawn from the re-run 'bomb scare' Grand National eventually won by Lord Gyllene.

At Aintree each year it is traditional for the senior steward to caution jockeys against setting off too fast. No such limitations seemed to have been put on McCoy for the summer and autumn of 1997, and by mid-December, as Will O'Hanlon reported, no record looked safe.

THE PHENOMENAL TONY McCOY ticked off another milestone yesterday, chalking up his 150th success of the season when Deano's Beeno, trained by Martin Pipe, took the Astbury Handicap Hurdle at Bangor.

The champion then rapidly moved on to 151 with the help of a former champion in Jonjo O'Neill, whose Jymjam Johnny made every yard of the running in the Bodfari Stud Handicap Chase.

O'Neill, mindful that his own career-best tally was 149 wins, was inevitably asked for his reflections on the fact hat someone had now passed that mark before Christmas. 'It's brilliant, times move on and it's good for the game that records continue to be broken,' he said.

'It's a hell of an achievement. You're up and down the country all the time. I remember from my time just how much all the travelling took out of me.'

Few of McCoy's 151 wins have been easier than that on the 2-9 shot Deano's Beeno, who saw off four rivals without breaking sweat.

McCOY'S SEASON 1996-1997	
wins:	190
rides:	666
strike rate:	29%
position in championship:	1st

McCoy, having received his now routine bottle of bubbly after yet another feat of record-breaking, was quick to thank Martin Pipe (who has provided 93 of this season's victories) for his part in the success story. 'They make the job easy, and here's hoping he can provide me with a few more steering jobs before the season's over,' he said.

McCoy has been struggling with a touch of flu for the last fortnight. 'I can't seem to shake it off.' he said, but he has not been tempted to take time off to get rid of it. 'We're going to get plenty of time off soon,' he added, with a sideways look at the worsening weather outside.

McCoy, who is systematically rewriting every riding record in jump racing's roll of honour, broke his own record for the fastest-ever century of wins when partnering Sam Rockett to victory at Newton Abbot on 5 November.

He ended last season with a career-best 190 wins, which – at his present strike-rate and given good luck and fair weather – he should reach well before the Cheltenham Festival. His obvious next target is to eclipse Peter Scudamore's all-time record of 221 wins in a season, set in 1987-88.

The inevitable question about beating Scudamore's record elicited the just-as-inevitable cautious response. 'There's a long way to go, but if I'm still in one piece after Cheltenham [in mid-March] then we'll see,' he said.

The numbers were fantastic, but at Cheltenham they came with performances to match – a table-topping and record-equalling five winners, and in Champleve's short-head victory over the Richard Dunwoody-ridden Hill Society in the Arkle there was a finish the two jockeys still talk about every time they meet. Or rather, McCoy wants to because Dunwoody was his 'Beau Ideal', and to beat him on the biggest stage of all was supremely satisfying.

Graham Dench saw one of the great Cheltenham finishes.

THE TWO outstanding jump jockeys of the present day fought out the closest Festival finish in years in yesterday's Guinness Arkle

Chase, and the only shame of it was that there had to be a loser. A dead-heat would have satisfied just about everybody.

The consensus of opinion in the grandstand after Champleve and Hill Society had passed the post locked together was that the latter, who had made up a good four lengths from the last, had prevailed, and initially they bet 1-4 Hill Society in the photo. Even Champleve's jockey Tony McCoy was convinced he'd been beaten.

Yet Richard Dunwoody on Hill Society was far from confident, declining to go into the winner's spot and venturing the opinion that McCoy had 'done' him on the line. Once the judge called for a print it was clear the result could go either way.

When it was eventually announced that Champleve, who had gone on at the seventh, had won by a short head there was still an element of disbelief, but Martin Pipe wasted no time in offering commiserations to his opposite number Noel Meade, embracing him warmly and telling the press he is not only 'a great trainer', but also 'a great man'.

Champleve, who had once beaten Pipe's Imperial Cup winner Blowing Wind in France, was a second successive Arkle winner for owner David Johnson as well as for Pipe and McCoy, following Or Royal. Johnson already topped the owners' table and his ambition to win the title looks ever more likely to succeed.

'A finish the two jockeys still talk about every time they meet.' AP on Champleve (far side) beats Richard Dunwoody on Hill Society by a short head in the Guinness Arkle Trophy at Cheltenham, 17 March 1998.

Pipe could hardly believe he had won, saying: 'That's amazing. I thought we were second, so I had no nerves at all watching the replay. I definitely would have settled for a dead-heat.

'It was a great finish to a great race, and they are two great jockeys, but I thought Champleve was tying up a bit up the hill and veering to the right. It's a great thrill to win the race twice, but I still want to see it again. I think I must need glasses!'

It was another superb effort from McCoy, who said afterwards: 'I was calling Dunwoody all sorts of names because I was sure we'd been beaten a short head. We're good friends, but great rivals, and I'd have been absolutely gutted if he'd beaten me a short head!'

Dunwoody's effort was arguably even better for, unlike Champleve, Hill Society was always struggling to go the pace, and at the top of the hill he was only seventh and looking a forlorn hope. However, Dunwoody kept pushing and shoving, and as Meade said: 'He flew up the hill, just like he did in last year's Champion Hurdle [in which he finished fifth].'

The winners were still coming at the flood, and only two weeks after Cheltenham Neil Morrice was reporting how a horse with the little name of Petite Risk took AP past Peter Scudamore's long thought unbeatable 221 winners record for a single season.

222 up: returning on Petite Risk, and (opposite) dowsing the crowd.

TONY McCOY had no sooner entered the record books at Ludlow yesterday as the man to have ridden the most winners in a season than his sights were set on new horizons and the possibility of breaking through the 250-winner barrier.

With ten weeks of the campaign still to go, and no sign of a let-up in the strike-rate of Martin Pipe's horses, McCoy can look to not only reaching 250 but going a fair way past it, providing he steers clear of injury.

However, he said the prospect of reaching 300 winners by the end of the season was 'completely out of the question'.

After returning to loud and warm applause from the crowd three-deep around the winner's circle after winner no. 222 on

Pipe's Petite Risk, McCoy said: 'Three hundred is a long way off and not a realistic target, but if I can keep it up and stay out of trouble, 250 or 260 winners could be a possibility by the end of May.

'I just need to keep riding good horses and for Martin's horses to stay well, as they have – touch wood – throughout the season.'

McCoy, who notched the record on his 712th ride of the season, took 49 more than Peter Scudamore (663) to get there. The achievement was only marginally faster than that of Scudamore's, as McCoy took 296 days whereas Scudamore took 309 days.

McCoy had to wait slightly longer than expected to break the record as he fully expected Doctoor to land the odds in the day's opening race.

Doctoor finished second, but an hour later McCoy was on board 8-11 chance Petite Risk in the Bundy (Europe) Juvenile Novices' Hurdle and the partnership never had an anxious moment.

After dismounting in the winner's enclosure, McCoy soaked the surrounding photographers and journalists with champagne as if he had just won a Formula One Grand Prix.

He said: 'I definitely can't believe it, it's like a dream come true. When I started riding for Toby Balding three and a half years ago, I just wanted to ride as many winners as possible. I couldn't imagine this would happen so quickly.'

But McCoy, still as modest as when he first came over from Ireland, displayed a hint of embarrassment that he'd been turned over on 30-100 Doctoor in the first race.

'I don't like getting beaten when I think I'm going to win, and Doctoor is a funny horse who found the track a bit tight and didn't jump especially well. That said, he was an odds-on shot and odds-on shots should win.

'There was no pressure out there but plenty of attention, and I wanted to get it out of the way. I knew this filly [Petite Risk] was all right. She's not the most beautiful in the world to look at, but she has plenty of heart. It's just brilliant to have beaten someone as brilliant as Scu.'

> 'By riding that bit shorter I can bring myself down to get hold of them better.'
>
> TONY McCOY

Asked at what stage of proceedings he felt the record was on, McCoy said: 'You don't really think it's on until you get past it, though I didn't think it could possibly happen as quick. What accelerated it was the fact that I had such a good Cheltenham, and I find Martin very easy to ride for.

'Hopefully Martin's horses will keep their form through Aintree but I've agreed that I'll take a break in June. I've never picked up a club before, but Brad [Graham Bradley] is organising a golf holiday and tells me I'm on it!'

This is what it felt like for me:

WE HAVE never seen his like before. Wrap up the record books, stow away the videos and start counting anew. What Tony McCoy is currently doing out there on the racetrack is something extra in every sense.

The new record he posted at Ludlow yesterday is just the latest chapter in a story which has unfolded so gloriously and so spectacularly over the past few years.

All a champion can do is to be dominant in his era and each great one has added a unique image of his own. My memories start with Fred Winter, short, square, clamped in and compulsive, his whole body forcing his horse forward in a way no one has ever witnessed since. What a privilege it was to have been beside the maestro as he powered down the hill at Cheltenham 35 years ago this April in his retirement season.

How lucky to have been around Mellor and Biddlecombe, who had their own claims to immortality. Stan, the thinking man's jockey, always ready to switch and change when even the horse thought all was lost. Terry, the blond bomber, who on his day had a dash and flair that no contemporary could match.

How fortunate to have delighted later in the astonishing balance and brains and side-splitting cheek that John Francome brought to the party. To have wondered at the McCoy machine in quite such extraordinary steel. And he is not 24 until May 4.

It's an enormous melting pot of experience for one still full of the dash of youth and out of it has come a rider who actually does it differently. This season he has pulled his leathers up to almost Flat-racing length, and far from putting him too high from the saddle it has actually made him neater and tighter when he lowers his body to drive a horse into an obstacle or force it to extra effort.

'Last season I felt I was still rather big on a horse, rolling round it a bit,' he said quietly last weekend. 'By riding that bit shorter I can bring myself down to get hold of them better.' These are perfectionist things, but at Cheltenham last week the watching world had to accept that perfection was hardly a length away.

Champleve and the great duel with Dunwoody, the sort of relentless finishing battle that only the Festival gives. Unsinkable Boxer, the hard-pulling 'certainty' who had to be held cool before playing the ace. Edredon Bleu, the all-the-way attack, Cyfor Malta the last-fence challenger, and finally the mighty gamble on Blowing Wind and the ruthless making up of the mind when the horse stalled on the final turn. Five different memories from the Cotswolds but McCoy branded into every one.

This is the criterion of greatness. The feel that only he can do it quite like this. Other jockeys have style and flair and strength, but let the images spin through your mind, and which is the one that is the most committed of them all?

A good three-quarters of a mile still to run at Uttoxeter last Saturday and McCoy did not so much send Nigel's Lad clear as personally demand him. On the face of it, this was just another front-running victory amongst so many, but as horse and rider bore down on us beside the last hurdle, you could see the compulsion in every stride, could notice in one instant just how the deed was done.

For while whip and voice and heel can send strong signals, the only actual way a horse can accelerate on the flat or over a jump is if he gets more thrust as his hind hooves bite the turf. As Nigel's

Overleaf: 'I really bonded with him – both of us wanted to win': AP and Pridwell lock horns with Champion Hurdle hero Istabraq (Charlie Swan) in the Martell Aintree Hurdle, 4 April 1998.

Lad thundered in and up and over, every ounce of McCoy's long, lean bodyweight thrust back and down the line. Man and horse leapt as one.

What he is doing is right on the edge of the line, right close to the horns of the bull. It is fuelled by the fearless, limitless energy of youth, as yet unslowed by the aches and fears that will one day come as surely as the evening dark. That's why it's so good to salute this moment. This time when our racetracks are lit by a wonder called Tony McCoy.

But whilst all this might thrill old lags like me, the sheer forcefulness of the finishing drive upset the authorities, who felt its use of the whip broke the guidelines they had produced to protect racing's image.

The first and most notorious case came in the race before the annual McCoy tilt at jumping's greatest prize. In that 1998 Grand National Challenger Du Luc fell with AP at the very first fence. In the preceding Aintree Hurdle the duel between Charlie Swan on Istabraq, who had just won the first of his three Champion Hurdles, and the McCoy-ridden Pridwell saw the latter get up in a photofinish amid such excitement that not only McCoy but a Racing Post *readers' poll voted it the finish of the season.*

But it also earned the jockey a four-day suspension – later extended to six on appeal – for using his whip with 'excessive force'. It was a boil of disagreement which grew as the months ticked by, and when the stewards intervened for a fifth time after McCoy won a little race on a rain-sodden day at Fontwell in November, the rider was so wound up that when he won the Murphy's Gold Cup on Cyfor Malta at Cheltenham that weekend he hurled his whip into the crowd with a look of almost demented defiance.

The issue of a champion jockey being fined for what he considered to be trying too hard was not something that could be easily resolved. But considerable efforts on either side, including a visit by McCoy to the British Racing School in Newmarket, began to get some sort of understanding, although there was a flare-up when owner David

Johnson said there was 'a witch hunt' after his jockey had been penalised at Sandown, and another when Jockey Club Director of Regulation Malcolm Wallace said, 'It ain't working for McCoy' after the jockey was banned after winning at Cheltenham.

By the time Alastair Down went to see AP with the result of that poll voting the Pridwell finish the best of the whole of 1998, the champion was in more constructive mood than most of us who wrote about it.

McCOY'S SEASON 1997-1998	
wins:	253
rides:	831
strike rate:	30%
position in championship:	1st

POPULAR OPINION is not infallible, but law-makers flout the will of the people at their peril. So the overwhelming verdict of *Racing Post* readers, that the finish Tony McCoy produced aboard Pridwell on Grand National day was the outstanding ride of 1998, is an unambiguous mass memo from the public to Portman Square.

From the moment the pair passed the post ahead of the great Istabraq, most on hand at Aintree were adamant they had witnessed something exceptional. The stewards thought otherwise, banning McCoy for four days – and another two days were added for good measure on appeal.

Clearly, readers of the *Post* concur with the view expressed in Timeform's *Chasers and Hurdlers* annual: 'It seems perverse to taint the memory of this stirring race by even giving the briefest mention here to the subsequent treatment by the stewards, interpreting the rule-book to the letter, of winning jockey Tony McCoy, who had, quite simply, ridden like a man inspired.'

Those who ignorantly dismiss McCoy as a one-dimensional beater of carpets should listen to him as he sits and calmly goes through a tape of the race.

'The ground was terrible,' he says, 'but Pridwell was always happy, because he was doing things at his own speed.

'I love riding him because you have to think on him and do everything you can to keep him thinking he's the bee's knees.

'As long as you can get there on him before you have to make him get there, you are all right.

'Four out he's upsides and loving it, and I just pull him back a touch. You have to get him to do it without bullying him – if you tried to force him to jump off, he'd just stand there, look round and say, "What do you think you're playing at?"

'Coming into the straight, I knew Istabraq was just behind me and so I just eased out a touch – I didn't mind Charlie having to go out into the middle of Aintree just a bit!

'He jumps the second-last and I'm pushing away, but I never touch him and in fact it isn't until we're headed on the run-in that I start to give him a smack and he really battles.'

McCoy was halfway up the run-in and a length down on the Champion Hurdler when he finally reached for the heavy manners. He hit Pridwell seven times with full force, the horse dug deep on the desperate ground and responded all the way to the line.

No unprejudiced observer could arrive at any other conclusion than that McCoy's exceptional strength galvanised Pridwell into winning a race that had looked lost.

McCoy says: 'He can be a funny horse, but to be fair to him, last year it was only in the Champion Hurdle that he was a monkey. At Aintree, I really bonded with him – both of us wanted to win.'

In the months since Aintree, racing has had to wrestle with the spectacle of its champion seemingly at loggerheads with the Jockey Club over the whip rules – an irresistible force meeting an immovable object.

The low point came when McCoy picked up a 14-day ban on the Monday after winning the Murphy's on Cyfor Malta. His punishment included a period of re-education to change his style – like trying to retrain a fighter pilot to be a balloonist.

He dismisses the idea that he has been persecuted, but says: 'They simply didn't understand and I think they were beginning to believe I didn't like horses and beat every one to within an inch of its life.

'I reached the stage where, if there had been another country where I could have got a good job, then I'd have gone.'

While he has recovered from that bleak period, he has yet to solve the principal problem – he hits them in the wrong place, it's against the rules and he hasn't yet managed to stop doing it.

He admits that he has found it difficult to unpick his instinctive way of riding, but he hasn't given up trying and says: 'When I move into my new house, I'm getting the most advanced mechanical horse available and Graham Bradley is going to show me how to do it – we'll just work and work until it's done.'

While *Post* readers don't have a monopoly of wisdom, they are no fools either, and understand that the whip issue is both vexing and vitally important.

In recognising the genius of McCoy at Aintree, they are perhaps sending out a second message: that if the authorities wish to impose their will on McCoy, they may have to take a leaf out of the champion's book on Pridwell – and get him to do it without bullying him.

To everyone's extreme relief, and to Graham Bradley and the mechanical horse's considerable credit, McCoy was largely able to put the whip issue behind him and to end the season in typical fashion, albeit punctuated with a bit of fun at Sandown.

AP and Graham Bradley in training for a charity bungee jump.

JUMPS CHAMPION Tony McCoy gleefully put one over Flat-race rival Frankie Dettori in a special charity match race before racing at Sandown on Saturday.

The Italian risked endless teasing from his colleagues after tasting defeat under his own code when McCoy claimed victory in the Tote Challenge, a two-horse event run over 10 furlongs.

With a strategy designed to distract Dettori, McCoy drew his opponent's attention to the Sandown fences in a light-hearted affair that resulted in his mount O'Garney Park beating Omar's Odyssey.

'I was trying to put him off a bit up the straight,' said McCoy after raising pounds £5,000 for jockey Eddie Leonard's daughter Kerrie, who sustained a spinal injury in a farming accident.

Dettori, who collected £1,000 for Direct Aid For Africa, said: 'My horse was placed so he ran well! It was good fun and a good giggle.'

The last three days of the jumping season included days at Cartmel and Uttoxeter. It was the week before the Derby and most readers would have hardly got to the race reports for stories about forthcoming fancies at Epsom. But if they did, they would have found the McCoy story as astonishing as ever – life at the very limit. Tom O'Ryan reported.

Tony McCoy gave the crowd a vivid illustration of his insatiable hunger for winners, his vast array of talents and his remarkable resilience to injury when achieving a double, punctuated by a crashing fall.

Quite how he emerged unscathed from the drilling he got from Chippewa at the seventh fence in the novices' chase remains a mystery, but the grass stain on McCoy's breeches was the only tell-tale reminder of his spill when he powered Sefton Blake to victory in the novices' handicap hurdle, completing a double initiated by the Martin Pipe-trained Imshishway.

And Graham Cunningham was at Uttoxeter two days later.

Martin Pipe chose to attend Uttoxeter from six meetings he had runners at, and celebrated securing his ninth trainers' championship with a treble supplied by Ballymaloe Boy, Fairy Knight and Auetaler.

Chasing debutant Ballymaloe Boy got the better of a duel with Monsieur Darcy as the pair drew well clear in the maiden chase.

Fairy Knight was all out to pip stablemate Born To Please in a valuable seller featuring six Pipe runners, while Auetaler was shouted to an easy victory in the novice hurdle by owners Robbie Fowler and Steve McManaman.

All three Pipe winners were partnered by Tony McCoy who, despite several suspensions this season, signs off more than 50 winners clear of Richard Johnson on 186.

The curtain comes down without him at Hexham today, but McCoy will remain on the go by flying to New York to ride the New Zealand-trained Eric The Bee in the Meadowbrook Hurdle at Belmont on Thursday.

Eric The Bee finished fifth.

The curtain may have come down on a comparatively difficult season but it was soon up again with his wagons really on a roll. The 1997-98 record of 253 seemed awesome at the time, now even that would be put aside. If winners were your game, McCoy was the name.

McCOY'S SEASON 1998-1999	
wins:	186
rides:	768
strike rate:	24%
position in championship:	1st

BEING CHAMPION

B y now we were getting to appreciate what was in our midst. But officials as well as journalists were still having trouble at handling the extremes of energy that AP was prepared to spend or what to do if he didn't. How about this problem in August 1999?

TONY McCOY picked up a three-day ban at Worcester on Saturday after the stewards found he had eased one of his mounts too soon.

The punishment, which came hard on the heels of a four-day suspension imposed on McCoy by the Bangor stewards for using his whip with excessive force the previous day, drew a bitter reaction from the champion jockey.

At Worcester, McCoy stood up in his irons on Galix, the 9-4 favourite for the Bob Champion Cancer Trust Selling Hurdle, after the mare made a tired blunder at the final flight.

He then eased Galix down to a walk, allowing Peter Pointer and Alwena to pass her on the run-in, so relegating her to sixth behind Barley Meadow.

The stewards were unimpressed with McCoy's explanation that Galix was a spent force and had nothing more to give, and suspended him for three days (August 19-21) for 'prematurely easing an unplaced horse and allowing it to coast home with no assistance.'

McCoy has no plans to appeal, but defended his riding, saying: 'I sat up on a horse that I'd been fairly hard on for two and a half to three furlongs, but was by now well beaten.

'I wanted to jump the last on her, but she fell through it and I basically pulled her up on the run-in after that.

'You only have to look at the form book to know Galix is a short runner. Once she's headed she stops, and it was a choice of easing down or pulling up. I can't see any point in appealing, but that doesn't mean I agree with the decision.'

McCoy added: 'Pretty soon I'll only have to walk on a racecourse to be done for something or other, as I got four days for using my whip with excessive force at Bangor and 24 hours later I'm given another three days for insufficient effort. Does that make any sense?'

Previous spread: Queen Mother Champion Chase at Cheltenham, 15 March 2000. Edredon Bleu (AP McCoy, stripes) leads Celibate (Mick Fitzgerald) at the third fence.

During the winter of 1999-2000 AP wrote a weekly column for us on the Racing Post, *and it could make hungry reading for those on a normal diet. Just in case you don't get the picture, remember that by now he was 5ft 10ins in his socks and would immediately tip 11st if he allowed himself a normal man's rations. A particularly uncompromising regime of wasting preceded his ride on Rodock in the Murphy's Draughtflow Handicap Hurdle at Cheltenham on 14 November 1999, and – as he was able to reflect later – the deprivation was rewarded.*

The face of wasting: AP before riding Rodock in the Murphy's Draughtflow Handicap Hurdle at Cheltenham, 14 November 1999.

I GOT DOWN to 10st to ride Rodock at Cheltenham last Sunday, and it was worth it as he won the big hurdle race in good style.

Of course, 10st is way below my natural weight of about 11st 7lb, and a lot of people have said I must be mad to starve myself, but it's not quite as bad for me as it may seem, and it is nothing like the hell I'd go through watching someone else ride Rodock to victory.

I have heard some say I'll be finished in 10 years if I continue to ride at low weights, but why should I be? In any case, I only do it four or five times a year, and I don't believe it affects me that much. I just want to ride more winners than anyone else.

For those interested about my diet, on the Thursday before Rodock's race I had a cup of tea when I got up, and then treated myself to a nibble of chocolate before racing. During the races I had a can of diet coke, and then nothing until I got home, when I had a piece of toast and a small amount of scrambled egg for supper. I finished with a tea before I went to bed.

On the Friday I did the same, although I left out supper, while on Saturday I had one slice of chicken in the afternoon. Eating apart, I run about two and a half miles a day with a sweatsuit on, and on the day of Rodock's race I drove to the races in the sweatsuit with the heater full on.

As I have said, it was worth it because Rodock won, and as usual the trainer found the right race for the right horse. It was a good performance by a novice, but Rodock had to win, really, if he was a horse with a future.

Cheltenham has been the stage for many of McCoy's greatest moments, and in December 1999 it was lit up by a treble which took him to a thousand winners over jumps – and he was still only 25. Richard Griffiths reported.

THE BURNING DRIVE and determination of Tony McCoy came to the fore at the end of racing at Cheltenham on Saturday as he reflected on becoming the youngest jockey to win 1,000 races over jumps – and in record time.

It took McCoy only five years and 95 days to reach the landmark – about half the time it took Peter Scudamore and Richard Dunwoody. But within hours of becoming only the fifth jump jockey to reach 1,000 wins, when Majadou gave him the middle leg of a treble, McCoy had put the momentous achievement behind him.

He admitted: 'It's brilliant to do it, but when I got beat on Far Cry, that's what brings it all back to you. I'd forgotten all about it by then.

'Winning is the only thing that matters. When you get beat, you just want to move on to the next race and go one better.'

The four-time champion said his early link-up with Martin Pipe had given him an edge over Scudamore and Dunwoody.

'I got a good job at a very early age, so the number of winners I was riding was always pretty high, which is something I don't think they had early on. I'm also very lucky to have Dave Roberts as my agent. He works his butt off and deserves as much credit as I do.

'Obviously I owe an awful lot to Martin Pipe – he's just so professional. And I really would like to thank all the lads in the yard for their help and expertise.'

McCoy, who said he did not expect '1,000 rides, let alone 1,000 winners' when he arrived in Britain in 1994, described the crowd's reaction to his triumph as 'unbelievable'.

He continued: 'It's very much appreciated from the punters – they keep racing going. If I can ride winners for them, it keeps me happy. I know the punters and racegoers get upset if I don't ride a winner but they're never as upset as I am, believe me!' He added: 'I suppose I'll be trying to beat Richard Dunwoody's jumps record [1,699]. Richard isn't finished yet but I'll be doing my best to beat him. However, the main priority for me will be to stay in one piece.'

Pipe is reluctant to separate McCoy, Dunwoody and Scudamore, but he described his current champion as 'unique … simply the best.' He added: 'Tony McCoy is some lad – he's just got everything. Look how determined he is with his weight. He doesn't drink. He doesn't even eat!

'He's relentless in his pursuit of winners, a great believer in himself. He transmits his confidence to the horses. They really run for him, he gives them such confidence. His schooling – it's fantastic, it really is. This is an incredible achievement for such a young lad.'

Pipe's principal owner, David Johnson, who said both trainer and jockey should have 'insatiable' as their middle names, said: 'The secret to a great jockey is winning on horses perhaps he shouldn't have. With Tony, you always have the feeling you've got a couple of pounds in hand.'

Even the sceptics could scarce forbear to cheer and when it came to jumping few were more sceptical than Flat aficionado Paul Haigh. This tribute, published in the Post *two days before the start of the new millennium, is all the better for the pain it seems to bring Paul in making it.*

RACING IS POSITIVELY crawling with sycophants and persons whose first instinct on observing any famous backside is to reach for the mistletoe. Someone has to provide a corrective, which is one reason why this column tries to refrain from excessive compliment – or even, some might say, basic civility.

But every now and then we find ourselves falling from our own low standards, and today is such a day as we can no longer avoid addressing ourselves to what is currently the most important question in jump racing. This is: what makes Tony McCoy so good?

> 'Look how determined he is with his weight. He doesn't drink. He doesn't even eat!'
>
> MARTIN PIPE

Convention suggests this may be a fairly presumptuous inquiry from one who occasionally has more trouble maintaining a seat on a bar stool than AP does on a steeplechaser at racing speed. But convention can go and stuff itself. It clearly helps, but it is not necessary to have attempted, at some time, to do what he does before you can comment on his abilities, anymore than it's necessary to have written a symphony before you can opine that Beethoven wasn't bad at it at all.

Anyone who's watched a bit of racing is entitled to a view and here's one coming up. See if you agree or not.

Obviously, there are basic qualities required of any jockey. Courage is a *sine qua non*. But so is balance; so is strength; so is timing; so's a fully functioning brain. Does McCoy have a weakness in any one of these basics?

His balance is immaculate, as he demonstrated for the thousandth time when not even looking like being dislodged from Buckland Lad, the first of his three winners on Tuesday, after that horse had made a blunder early on that would have put most jockeys on the floor.

His strength in a finish requires no comment except that, in living memory anyway, there has never been a jump jockey you would want to put up against him if they were head to head on horses who both had about the same amount to give. The stewards have done their best to try to reduce him to the ranks. Thank God they have failed, cry his fans.

His timing doesn't get so much attention, largely because it's a quality that's not so ostentatiously on display. But watch him in any race and see how, and when, he chooses to attack; see how he goes for the opposition at the very moment they would like it least; see how he takes them on just as they're looking for a breather before their final effort or just after they've made a tiny but detectably weakening mistake. Only a rider with a brain that works efficiently – and all the time – can do that with any consistency. McCoy seems to have reached a stage now where he never, ever misses that sort of a trick.

What do you want to read about his courage? Quite right – nothing at all. Everybody knows he will drive any horse at any fence at any time. McCoy sit tight and hope to pop one just to be on the safe side? Per-lease!

Maybe it's all to do with his confidence. Maybe it's not so much bottle as an unshakeable conviction that he can handle anything this sport can throw at him. (I hope that writing this isn't going to tempt fate into sending him some freak disaster). Whatever the reason, there is no hint of trepidation in anything he ever does between the moment the tapes go up and the moment the winning post is reached.

Ask most punters to name McCoy's defining characteristic, though, and they will almost certainly say it's his determination. One of the greatest things about him is that he accepts defeat when he has to more slowly and more grudgingly than any jockey we have ever seen.

And one of the most extraordinary things about him – although perhaps not quite so extraordinary when you remember that so many of his mounts are trained by Martin Pipe – is the number of times his persistence pays off. Try and count the number of victories McCoy has conjured out of horses others would have allowed to come home in their own time. Don't bother with them all, or break for tea if you start to find yourself getting a bit tired.

But there is another characteristic of this man that is, if anything, an even more important ingredient in his unparalleled success. It is that every time he goes out to ride, he expects to win.

He doesn't just go out in hope. He goes in expectation – and you can almost feel his indignation if the horse fails to respond. Above all, I think this is what sets him apart from the rest.

More often than not, horses do what he asks of them. You can actually see their anxiety to satisfy him, or at least to obey. People have talked a lot about the mental communication between man and beast.

Here it is in action.

Is all that sycophancy? I hope not. I think it's just unvarnished truth.

> 'Every time he goes out to ride, he expects to win.'
>
> PAUL HAIGH

65

Haigh need not have worried about beating himself up over McCoy, because the harshest critic of the by then only four-times champion jockey continued to be himself. In January 2000 it was starvation down to 10st again, to ride Nordance Prince in the Victor Chandler Chase at Ascot.

Afterwards it was Alastair Down shaking the head in wonder.

OPEN UP the bumper box of clichés and hand me a shovel – it's that man McCoy again. Running to the last in Saturday's Victor Chandler Chase, it looked like the wasting time had been a waste of time as only the most cock-eyed optimist could have believed that Nordance Prince could be brought back to beat the bulk of Flagship Uberalles.

But, flying to the final fence, there came a moment when you could almost see McCoy say to himself, 'I haven't lived on fresh air, Red Bull and a daily lettuce leaf just to get done on this thing' and dig once more for victory.

Victor Chandler Chase, Ascot, 15 January 2000: AP and Nordance Prince just headed by Joe Tizzard and Flagship Uberalles at the last.

All week McCoy's fast in the fast lane had been monitored in the press; the next person whose weight is likely to be of such public interest will probably be the Blair baby.

I am unable to offer any serious insight into draconian weight-loss regimes – you might as well ask Bill Gates about selling the Big Issue – but McCoy is an expert.

Yesterday he said: 'It's never easy, but I find I can get down to 10 stone without too much trouble. But I have to say the last three or four pounds after that is pure hell, so it is.

'Breaking the 10-stone barrier may be a mental thing, I'm not sure, but it had to be done because this horse had to win if he was even to warrant an entry in the Champion Chase.

'Going to the last I said to myself, 'What sort of bloody idiot am I going to look if I get beat?' and so I thought, 'Well, we'll have another go.'

Don't run away with the simplistic idea that Nordance Prince's win was all down to McCoy. Flagship Uberalles wasn't fluent enough at the last, and that gave McCoy the chink of weakness that helped to make the 24lb weight difference decisive.

'In all fairness,' said McCoy, 'I didn't really go for him until after the second-last and I knew he'd stay on.

'But that second is some horse, and there's no way he's going backwards. I'm afraid none of us will beat him at Cheltenham.'

That is, of course, the lesson to take home from Ascot. Flagship Uberalles is still improving, and who is to say that the ratchet of his ability can't be raised another click or two yet?

He has had two pulverising races in a row but has risen to both occasions and, as Paul Nicholls said: 'He was supremely fit today, and if they're fit they get over it.'

You would have to strap two of his half-brother, Viking Flagship, together to make a Flagship Uberalles, but in other telling respects the genes run true. Just like that Flagship, this Flagship is a fighter and oozes attitude. You might not walk a mile in pinching brogues to take the 7-4 for Cheltenham, but you can't argue with his supremacy in the market.

We now have favourites ranging from warm to searing for four of the great pots at the Festival – Decoupage in the Arkle, Saturday's unflinching second in the Champion Chase, See More Business for the Gold Cup and the great in green and gold for the Champion Hurdle. How many of that fearsome foursome will prevail, I wonder?

But to return to Saturday; poor old Victor Chandler had just recovered from flu, only to catch a cold at Ascot as he had laid the winner at 8-1 and 6-1. There really is no gratitude in this world.

The man he has to blame is McCoy. My immediate post-race reaction was that no-one else would have won on the horse. That may be fanciful in view of the weight concession, and you may be astonished to hear that McCoy himself confided to someone that he thought he was 'crap'.

You wouldn't mind seeing the man when he thinks he's ridden a good one.

As for the weight loss, he is a professional jockey to whom the occasional period of spartan denial is part of the deal.

But the last time he did 10st – for Rodock on a Sunday at Cheltenham – he told me that when he got to Folkestone the following Thursday he arrived on course at 10st 10lb.

I don't know how much research has been done on the long-term effects on jockeys of see-sawing weight, but that sort of fluctuation on an already lean frame may take its toll.

McCoy casts a long shadow; take him out of the jockeys' table and we would all be eulogising about the young and exceptionally good Richard Johnson.

I'm the last person to want to corral McCoy or restrict the range of his brilliance. What I want to do is see the man give himself the chance of a long shelf-life in what is a uniquely demanding sport both physically and mentally.

His motto is 'thou shalt not lose' but he will eventually have to make choices for his own self-preservation, in both mind and body, about such matters as doing 10st.

Less haunted and harried than a year ago, sure in his own mind of the public's genuine warmth towards him, McCoy is becoming a better advert for the sport month by month. But if we are to enjoy him for years and years, he will have to learn to spare himself on occasions, to give himself a long future of saying yes.

On Saturday night Tony flew out for his Dad's 60th birthday celebrations. The best present he could give him – and us – would be still to be shredding records and warming up the winter when his old man is approaching 70.

A full decade on, the son-to-father present Alastair wished for the McCoys has duly been delivered. But the suggestion of 'sparing himself' has hardly been heeded – as the next record was to show. At Sandown on 18 February 2000, AP nursed an exhausted Mr Cool up the final hill. It was the champion's 200th winner of the season. All bets were off.

The following day, the Post *reported how the deposed record-holder had reacted.*

PETER SCUDAMORE, whose record-breaking exploits as a jump jockey are being fast eclipsed by Tony McCoy, led the tributes to his successor yesterday.

Until the emergence of McCoy, Scudamore had been the only jockey to ride 200 winners in a jumps season.

He said: 'People said they thought my score would never be beaten when I did it. It's a wonderful performance.

'I don't think McCoy will ever be beaten. He is just extraordinary.

'People say it's much easier to do these days, but the winners still have to be ridden and you can still lie under a fence while 30 others gallop over you. It's a remarkable record.'

Scudamore was joined in his praise of McCoy by another former champion, Terry Biddlecombe, who said: 'He's a quite superb jockey. He's never beat and I'm glad I wasn't riding against him as he might have been too good for me.

'It's quite amazing. I think I was the first jockey to ride 100 winners in consecutive seasons and I thought that was an achievement. Now he's doing double that.'

> 'People say it's much easier to do these days, but the winners still have to be ridden and you can still lie under a fence while 30 others gallop over you.'
>
> PETER SCUDAMORE

Michael Caulfield, executive manager of the Jockeys' Association, said: 'I was at Towcester when Scu did it but that was the end of April. Even then we thought it was an extraordinary achievement.

'But 200 in a season is almost the norm now for Tony. It's remarkable.'

Owner Peter Deal, for whom McCoy won the Champion Hurdle on Make A Stand, said: 'That 200th win on Mr Cool showed McCoy at his best.

'He nursed the horse home. He was in the right place at the right time. It was vintage McCoy and the perfect way to bring up the record.'

BHB senior jumps handicapper Phil Smith feels that McCoy wins races that other jockeys would not.

'It's not just the sheer quantity that's so remarkable,' Smith said. 'Within those 200 there are probably 30 or 40 that nobody else would have won on. Spring Saint at Taunton on Thursday was a good example. He carried it home.'

Trainer Josh Gifford said: 'It's a fantastic achievement and he's a nice lad to go with it. I must admit I never thought Jonjo O'Neill's record of 149 would be beaten, but records are there to be broken and times change.'

McCoy's Cheltenham Festival 2000 had a soaring high and a devastating low. The high, Edredon Bleu's brilliant victory in the Queen Mother Champion Chase, still blazes in the memory. Post reporter Jon Lees was on the spot.

TERRY BIDDLECOMBE produced the gameplan and Tony McCoy executed it to perfection to deliver an emotional Queen Mother Champion Chase victory for Edredon Bleu yesterday.

Three times champion jump jockey in the 1960s, Biddlecombe shared tears of joy with his wife and winning trainer Henrietta Knight and owner Jim Lewis at the fulfilment of a year-long ambition.

Opposite: Queen Mother Champion Chase, Cheltenham, 15 March 2000: already an epic encounter as Edredon Bleu (left), Direct Route and the obscured Flagship Uberalles take the last.

For McCoy, the triumph, in what he regards as 'the professionals' race', was one he had desired more than any other. 'Of all the races in the world, this was the one I wanted to win most of all,' he said.

But a vintage two-mile championship, in which victory over Direct Route was assured only after a photo-finish, was marred by a whip referral for Norman Williamson, the rider of the runner-up.

Williamson risks missing part of the Martell Grand National meeting as a result of being referred to Portman Square for hitting his mount across the ribs.

In Call Equiname's absence, Edredon Bleu and Direct Route, second and third last year, had a prime opportunity to claim the vacant crown.

But the substantial obstacle of Flagship Uberalles, who had dominated the division to date, stood in their way.

McCoy was employed to lead from the front, though not in tearaway style. Nordance Prince was on his heels when falling four out and impeding Space Trucker. But three out, the pressure was being applied by Flagship Uberalles and Direct Route.

Flagship Uberalles was untidy at that fence, then blundered the next and had nothing left for the finish. Edredon Bleu and Direct Route pulled away for an epic duel to the line decided by only a short head to complete the race in course-record time.

Biddlecombe, who never won the race as a jockey, said: 'This beats everything. Hen gave the orders when Edredon Bleu was beaten at Sandown and got it wrong. So Tony and I talked the tactics today and it worked.

'Edredon Bleu jumped unbelievably and saw some long strides, but Tony held onto him a bit longer today.

'It's a long way from the dip at the bottom of the hill to the winning post and I was feeling for Tony. Halfway up the run-in I thought he was beat, but Tony got after him again and just got up. He's the most exceptional jockey. He's greedy to ride winners; he's quite brilliant. I reckon he's about 1lb in front of me!'

Knight, who crowned a great day by winning the Royal & SunAlliance Chase with Lord Noelie, could not bring herself to watch the race. She did not speak to McCoy before the race and declined to leg him into the saddle.

'I was on the bank under the number-board and could hear the commentary,' she said.

'I came back to hear a photo-finish called and thought we'd been beaten again. When number three was called I couldn't believe it.

'This was the race we'd had in mind all year. Once we were beaten last year we decided to come back and try again. The horse was very, very well, spot-on for the day, and the more the ground dried out, the more we rejoiced. He loves to bounce off the surface.'

Lewis, who had finished third in the race with Nakir in addition to last year's second, said: 'I'm so pleased because Tony McCoy believed in this horse. He told me after we'd been stuffed at Sandown that this horse would win the Queen Mother. I told him, "I'll keep you to that."

'I thought we were going to lose in the same fashion as last year, when he jumped the last in front and got pegged back on the run-in.

'But McCoy is the Messiah. He sets my horse on fire.'

The 99-year-old Queen Mother herself presented McCoy with his prize. A day later a much younger life was cruelly snuffed out. AP had been suspended when Gloria Victis was so sensational a victor of the Racing Post Chase under Richard Johnson at the end of February that connections decided to pitch him at the Gold Cup itself.

McCoy was thrilled by that decision, and eight days before the Gold Cup had written in his column:

I WAS AS EXCITED as most racing fans to learn yesterday that Gloria Victis will be going for the Tote Cheltenham Gold Cup next week – now I just hope he wins.

It can't have been an easy decision for Martin Pipe or owner Terry Neill to make – obviously, the Royal & SunAlliance Chase presented a much easier opportunity.

'McCoy is the Messiah. He sets my horse on fire.'

JIM LEWIS

73

But they've opted to go for Gold, and no horse in the Gold Cup will be more on the upgrade than Gloria Victis is at the moment.

I saw him yesterday morning and, touch wood, he continues to look really well and is in great shape.

As anyone who reads my column knows, I was far from surprised at the way he won the Racing Post Chase at Kempton. He had to win like that to have a chance in the Gold Cup.

But he is a very good horse, and I've got no worries about going left-handed at Cheltenham.

I know he jumped right on his first run at Newbury and they say that he did at Auteuil as well. But I thought he went a bit left at Kempton, so maybe he's just that type of horse.

Obviously he's been tried on pretty flat tracks so far, but he should be fine going up and down the hills at Prestbury Park, and I'm sure he'll stay the trip very well.

Only what happens a week tomorrow will tell us whether Gloria Victis has the class to win a Gold Cup.

But he's done nothing to suggest that he's anything other than very, very good, and I'll be doing my best to get him home in front.

Hopefully, it will take a very good one to catch us.

But, as we reported the day after the race, it didn't work out.

CHAMPIONS MARTIN PIPE and Tony McCoy were last night trying to come to terms with the death of Gloria Victis, whose exciting chasing career was cruelly extinguished during the climax to the Tote Cheltenham Gold Cup.

Together with owner Terry Neill, they mourned the Racing Post Chase winner, who suffered such severe injuries in a fall at the second last that he had to be put down.

Gloria Victis had helped establish the race as a spectacle. He was able to make much of the running, despite jumping to the right at every fence, in an audacious bid to claim the sport's greatest chasing prize at the tender age of six.

Tote Cheltenham Gold Cup, 16 March 2000: Gloria Victis (AP) leads See More Business (Mick Fitzgerald) on the first circuit.

He had just been headed by Looks Like Trouble and Florida Pearl when he crashed heavily to the ground, fracturing his near-fore cannon bone so seriously that he could not be saved.

A tearful Pipe, who had committed his star novice to the Gold Cup only a week earlier instead of the Royal & SunAlliance Chase, said: 'In my view Gloria Victis was a Gold Cup winner – that is what he meant to me.

'He's one of the most exciting horses I've trained and it will be hard to go round evening stables at Pond House tonight without him there.

'He proved in the Racing Post Chase what a great jumper he was, and he was one of those horses that captured the public's imagination very quickly.

'I'd like to thank everyone who has patted me on the back. It doesn't bring the horse back, but it's nice to know that people care.'

McCoy was distraught at the loss of a horse who within four months had established himself as an outstanding novice.

He said: 'I'm mortified. Gloria Victis is one of the most exciting horses I've ever sat on and I've really fallen in love with him.

'We were pulling our hair out, having failed to land a race. It really had got to us – winning at Cheltenham means everything.'

TONY McCOY

'Anyone who reads the Racing Post will know what I feel about the horse and what happened today is a tragedy for his owner and trainer.'

Vets were at Gloria Victis's side within seconds of his fall to administer painkillers, and the horse got up to hobble into the horse ambulance to be taken for treatment in the veterinary centre at the racecourse stables.

Peter Webbon, the Jockey Club's chief veterinary officer, said: 'He fractured the bottom end of the cannon bone but there were complications because the sesamoid bones were also damaged and there was extensive soft-tissue damage.

'Initially there was a reasonable chance that it would be amenable to surgical repair. But the more opportunity the vets had to examine it fully, the more it emerged that it was not a treatable injury.

'His owner and trainer were determined to do everything that could be done to try to save the horse, but there are some injuries that cannot be treated.

'It would have been almost an explosive injury on the impact of the fall, that is why there was so much disruption of the structure.

'The damage was so extensive and would have taken so long to repair that the quality of life for the horse would not have been good enough to justify saving him.

'Serious injury to such a well-known horse is bound to attract attention, but the first two days of the Festival have been virtually injury free, due to the brilliant condition of the course, the obstacles and the horses – which are a credit to everyone involved.'

Gloria Victis, the latest recruit from the French production line that Pipe has found so rewarding, burst on to the chasing scene at the Newbury Hennessy meeting, when he won his first start in Britain over fences.

He suffered defeat on his next start at Sandown, but his real ability emerged when he was moved up to three miles to record a spectacular wide-margin win in the Feltham Novices' Chase at Kempton.

But it was another stunning performance in capturing the Racing Post Chase, when he came very close to beating the six-minute barrier despite soft ground and the burden of top weight, which earned him the reputation of being the most exciting steeplechaser in training.

That week's McCoy column was one of the most bitter-sweet of all.

THE FEELING I had on Thursday could hardly have been more different than the one I had the previous afternoon.

Then, of course, I landed the Queen Mother Champion Chase on Edredon Bleu and was on cloud nine.

The Queen Mother's race was the one I really wanted, as it's the fastest two-mile race in the world, and to win it you have to get everything perfect.

Edredon Bleu had been prepared to perfection by Henrietta Knight and he jumped brilliantly. He was a bit like Gloria Victis at two-mile pace.

It's so exciting riding a horse you can throw at every fence and know he'll take off for you. Edredon Bleu went for it, and so did I, and it paid off.

Receiving a prize from the Queen Mother was one of the best moments in my career. She's an incredible lady and I hope I'll be meeting her in similar circumstances on plenty more occasions.

I got the better of Norman Williamson in the tight finish, and the result did have its ironies.

Earlier that afternoon, Norman had landed the Royal & SunAlliance Novices' Hurdle on Monsignor, which was his first victory of the meeting. Edredon Bleu had also got me off the mark.

It was ironic because on Tuesday evening, Norman and I had gone out for dinner, and we didn't say much after a blank day. We sort of just sat there looking at each other.

In fact, we were pulling our hair out, having failed to land a race. It really had got to us – winning at Cheltenham means everything.

In the end, we had to tell each other to pull ourselves together, and Norman pointed out there were still two days to go, even though it felt like the end of the world. Perhaps, judged on what happened on Wednesday, someone, somewhere, took pity on us.

Incidentally, Norman and I made a pact that if we both failed to win anything we'd go to the winner's enclosure after the County Hurdle and just sit there. Fortunately, that wasn't necessary.

The next season the McCoy column moved to better-paid pastures at the Daily Telegraph*, but that winter showed glimpses of the man behind the ruthless competitor, the guy who, to the surprise of many, also likes seeing the funny side.*

A 15-YEAR-OLD CAMEL guest-starring at Ascot managed to do what so few horses have achieved – unseat Tony McCoy!

But the champion jockey had the last laugh as he had already driven out Atakor in typical style to defeat his 20-year-old rival Teifet, the mount of Mick Fitzgerald.

The match was organised as a trial for a camel race at the Lambourn Open Day on Good Friday.

Under inspired riding, the pair did battle over the final furlong of the Flat course before a small but appreciative crowd.

'I expect him to get a stiff fine.' AP and Atakor resist the challenge of Teifet and Mick Fitzgerald.

McCoy, who was unshipped shortly after the finishing line when his camel decided to turn sharply right, quipped: 'It was very interesting, and as far back as I've ever sat on an animal.

'I didn't have much steering and I didn't have much control – that's why I fell off! But I always had the race in safe-keeping and Fitzy never had a chance.'

Fitzgerald added: 'It was a good crack but, as usual, AP jumped the start – I expect him to get a stiff fine.'

McCOY'S SEASON 1999-2000	
wins:	245
rides:	803
strike rate:	31%
position in championship:	1st

A series of injuries, including an injured shoulder and thumb when falling on the Martin Pipe-trained favourite Dark Stranger in the Grand National, meant that the 1999-2000 season did not finally match the record-breaking 253 of two years before. Not exactly bad, though.

In the autumn of 2000 Richard Dunwoody's absorbing autobiography Obsessed *came out, and with it the controversial – and certainly book-selling – opinion that Peter Scudamore was 'a stronger jockey' than AP McCoy. It was a cue for one of Paul Haigh's most stylish turns.*

THE LEAVES DRIFT from the withering stump of the Flat season. Autumnal deluges pulp form books as massive fields of mediocrities turn mile-long straights into mud. The morning chorus yields to the grisly sounds of giggling bookies and – what's this? – our old chum Seasonally Affected Depression crooks cruel claws at those of us too dumb or just too cussed to desist on this, the dreaded punting cusp.

Gulp.

What we need is a nice, big jumps-related talking point. How very kind of Richard Dunwoody to have provided the very thing.

For those still unaware of it, the former champion jockey has published an autobiography. Appropriately entitled *Obsessed*, it charts the total subordination of his private life to his professional.

Like all good memoirs, it also offers the occasional chunk of controversy, and none could be meatier than his insistence that his old rival Peter Scudamore was 'a stronger jockey' than – I tremble a little even to repeat this – the great and, as most of us are now convinced, unparalleled AP McCoy.

Obviously, it would be fairly easy to scoff at such a claim and put it down to the desire we all feel sometimes to aggrandise our contemporaries at the expense of upstart parvenus. But such is Dunwoody's candour elsewhere in the book, and such is his own right to be considered an authority, that we have to take the claim seriously.

The reluctance to do so stems not from disrespect for Scu who, lest we forget, inspired in his time almost the same awe as his successor does now, but from a reluctance to consider the possibility that any jockey could ever have been stronger than McCoy.

Better maybe. If that had been Dunwoody's claim we could at least have understood it, although we would no doubt have rejected it out of hand. But stronger? The idea just does not make sense.

In what way could Scu ever have been stronger than AP? Did he start riding finishes earlier? How could he possibly have done so when McCoy is famous for beginning his demands sometimes with a whole circuit to go?

Was he more vigorous with the whip? Well, Scu operated in less fastidious times, so perhaps that is just conceivable. But sit them both down on a recalcitrant who still has something to give and let them know that (avert your gaze please if you are of sensitive nature or delicate constitution) they may deal with him as they think fit, and it is surely beyond the bounds of credibility that anyone would emerge as a sterner disciplinarian than McCoy.

What about will? Is that what Dunwoody means? Is he saying that anyone who ever rode over jumps had a more powerful will than McCoy, or a grimmer determination to bend a horse to it? Because if he is, then that's almost fighting talk these days in the betting shops and on the racecourses. No-one makes up horses' minds for them like McCoy, and no-one has. These are not just vague opinions. These are articles of faith.

But Dunwoody, as anyone with a memory of his riding in his prime would expect, sticks to his guns. What he is saying, he insists, is that if he were a horse who did not feel much like running, he would rather be ridden by McCoy than Scudamore.

Now, obviously we are not going to get a definitive judgement on this from anyone, except perhaps Mister Ed. But if this is really the basis of his argument, it does not sound like a great compliment to the past master.

There are still plenty of people who will not let McCoy anywhere near one of their horses, simply because they think he demands too much.

They think he breaks as many as he makes – although no-one has produced statistics to support that claim. Cast your mind back a decade and you realise they sometimes said the same about the then champ. So maybe, when you think about it, there is not that much between them in terms of sternness.

One suspects that the pair are/were fitter than most who have ever ridden. But still that does not bring us any nearer to concluding the argument.

What does, perhaps, are Scu's own words. Speaking very graciously on television on Sunday about the man so many think has taken over his mantle as the most effective jump jockey there has ever been, he was eloquent in explaining how McCoy – by leaning forward, by riding more aggressively into the obstacles, by going for injections of pace where others would relax or take a pull – has changed the whole nature of jump race-riding. What he might have added is that Richard Johnson has learned that, if he is to compete, he has got to do the same. But that will do for me.

If I were a horse, I would not want to argue with Scudamore. To half-quote Muhammad Ali, I would wake up and apologise if I even dreamed about arguing with McCoy.

In fact, by the McCoy standards what followed was not the greatest season 'slumping' (if we can indulge in the word) from 245 to 191 winners. The mitigating circumstances included the normal injuries

> 'Peter Scudamore was eloquent in explaining how McCoy – by leaning forward, by riding more aggressively into the obstacles, by going for injections of pace where others would relax or take a pull – has changed the whole nature of jump race-riding.'
>
> PAUL HAIGH

plus a month off with concussion, a bizarre suspension for 'verbal abuse of his horse' after finishing second at Southwell, the foot-and-mouth outbreak which eliminated the Cheltenham Festival, and a Grand National run in ground so desperate that Alastair Down made a case that the race should never have been run at all – a suggestion which brought all manner of opprobrium down on his head. McCoy's horse Blowing Wind had been going well when flattened by a loose horse early on the second circuit, but with his characteristic never-say-die spirit AP remounted and slogged round to finish third, way behind the winner Red Marauder and one of only four finishers.

When he talked to Alastair just before the end of term he was happily keen to get that season into perspective.

AP McCOY is in flying form: 'You're taking some flak! I thought I'd had a bad Grand National and at one point I thought I was going to win the thing. But, Jaysus, you had an even unluckier run and never had a hope of winning it.

'I played golf with Francome this morning and as soon as I saw him I said, "Oh God, I've forgotten to ring Alastair," and he says, "Don't worry, I'll ring him later and wind him up that you're another one not talking to him."'

All this is delivered with the customary gales of McCoy laughter and the fact is that this chomper of record books, who has looked driven to the point of haunted on occasions in the saddle, is extremely good company out of it, and no fool either.

'It's been a disastrous season,' he says, 'and I can't wait until it's over. I could have won the National, as he was running away. Aintree was desperate and I've never had a worse meeting in my life.

'My aim this year had been to ride 200 winners but I'll need five on Monday if I'm going to get near it. Mind you, I'd ride 20 horses a day if I could, but it's not possible.'

Plenty have worried about McCoy burning out, me included, but we fail to appreciate how much effort goes into him having nothing else to concern him beyond riding.

He says: 'I don't have a lot to worry about – no wife or children and I don't have to ride out much. Having Gee Armytage working here is a huge help and means I can totally focus on the races.

'Things are made as easy as possible and I have a better chance of lasting than people think.'

McCoy is a legendary man for his row of zeds. He makes Rip Van Winkle look like a catnapper and if they ever did a remake of The Big Sleep then McCoy would make a perfect Humphrey Bogart.

He says: 'On a Sunday, I wouldn't get out of bed at all if I didn't have to. I'd just lie there being useless all day.

'People forget that I love what I do. How can you burn out doing something you've wanted to do since you were a child? I'd do it for fun, do it for nothing.

'I don't have any fear of failure, but you have to live with the fact of failure because it does get to the stage when you think you can't be seen not to be winning.

Martell Grand National, 7 April 2001: the never-say-die spirit of AP on Blowing Wind (left) and Ruby Walsh on Papillon. Both horses having been remounted, they finished third and fourth respectively behind Red Marauder and Smarty.

'But even when it does depress you or get you down, you still appreciate the job. Some may look into my eyes and see no lights on, but it will be a great pleasure to prove them wrong. They'll have a hard time trying to burn me out.'

Five years ago, McCoy would not have even acknowledged the existence of burnout, but he has changed greatly. Look at his relaxed and communicative manner in front of a camera, the way he has battled through his problems with the whip and the impression he gives of being much more at ease with himself.

He says: 'One day I'd like to be like Richard Dunwoody and ride just the good ones. But that's still a long way off as I value the prestige of being champion and that means more to me than winning the big races.

'A lot of the lads don't understand Richard's attitude to racing at the moment, but I do totally. He was absolutely brilliant and now he can't do it any more – can't even bring himself to buy a racing paper. I just hope he finds what he's looking for.'

A major key to McCoy's success is not just that he rides for Martin Pipe but that the two actually work well together; their wavelengths are in tune.

He says: 'A lot of the lads have found it hard working for Pipey but I do genuinely get on with the man. We have our rows, but he's a legend and nothing really fazes him.

'People don't realise the work – and the work in depth – he puts into it. It's not about galloping them 50 times a day, he's fascinated by the mental side.'

McCoy adds: 'Any health and fitness programme on the TV and he's watching it. He wants to know what made Ali so exceptional, how Emil Zatopek could sprint after all that distance and what turned Linford Christie from being average into an Olympic champion. Most of all, he wants to know why he can't do the same with some selling hurdler!'

It isn't all plain sailing with Pipe, but the two are bound by mutual respect and a passion for winners. McCoy is not an easy man to get roused, but I suspect he stays roused when he feels slighted.

He is scathing of one Lambourn trainer he will no longer ride for, not for the fact of being jocked off one but, as he says: 'He never said "boo" to me after the race or at any other time. But he told everyone else I'd made a bollocks of it. It was the way he did it that annoyed me, the principle of it, if you like.'

'Given what you put into a ride, it's hard not to hold a grudge when someone jocks you off, hard to accept it. And there's no need to come running back two months later expecting me to forget it.'

But the most difficult relationship for McCoy has been with the authorities.

A couple of years ago we were in the unworkable situation of having an outstanding champion forever falling foul of the rules. Something had to be done and there has been a lot of work put in by both McCoy and some key sympathetic figures at the Jockey Club.

McCoy says: 'I was hitting them too many times for the guidelines, but the bigger problem was that the way I taught myself to use the whip means I catch horses short sometimes.

'I feel I'm in a better rhythm when I'm catching them short, and Norman Williamson has much the same problem.

'But I am a much better rider than four years ago, better than in the days of Mr Mulligan and Make A Stand. A lot of little loose things are tighter and stronger now.

'I haven't been done for frequency for two years. I used to be frightened that, if I got beat, people would think I wasn't strong enough. But I've improved in my mind and realise I can be every bit as strong without giving them a smack.

'I've learned what a horse can give and what I can get out of it.'

It took this observer longer than it should have done to appreciate McCoy's qualities as a jockey, that there was more to him in the saddle than mere statistics.

But just as important is that, complicated in an uncomplicated sort of way, he's a sound man who has got a grip on his life and how to lead it. You'd need a fair pile of sleepers to burn this fellow out.

'I've learned what a horse can give and what I can get out of it.'

TONY McCOY

85

McCOY'S SEASON 2000-2001	
wins:	191
rides:	775
strike rate:	25%
position in championship:	1st

The fastest century: AP and Present Bleu cruise home to win the Sussex County Cricket Club Claiming Hurdle at Plumpton, 17 September 2001.

By the end of April 2001 McCoy had landed his seventh consecutive championship. By September 2001 we could feel the momentum was greater than ever. Graham Dench reported yet another new record.

TONY McCOY shattered his previous best time for 100 winners in a season at Plumpton yesterday – and immediately set himself new goals, including winning all the races at the Cheltenham Festival.

The champion jumps jockey spoke of his enduring passion for the sport and said that he continues to relish every ride.

Yesterday's fastest century, which came via what he described as an 'armchair ride' on his boss Martin Pipe's Present Bleu in the claiming hurdle, was arrived at in a time some seven weeks quicker than his previous best, which was achieved on 5 November 1997. It is a remarkable achievement, even allowing for the fact that the season starts earlier now – on 30 April this year compared with 5 June in 1997.

McCoy said: 'I am very lucky. I have a great job – it's a great way to earn a living. I couldn't think of a job I'd want to do any more than the one I'm doing now – that's probably why I enjoy riding so much.

'I'm lucky I ride such good horses and ride those winners.

'The main thing is to get to the races and ride horses that are faster than everyone else's. That's what makes it exciting.'

Reflecting on the achievement, McCoy recognised the contribution of Pipe and Dave Roberts, the jockey's agent.

'It was quick,' he said. 'I would obviously like to thank my agent for doing such a great job, and, of course, the trainer – 70 per cent of the winners have been for him, so you could say he helped a little bit!'

McCoy, deprived of a double century last season by the foot-and-mouth epidemic – his final total was 191 – now hopes to beat his previous best of 253 victories in a season, and also numbers a win in the Grand National as an ambition alongside a Cheltenham full house.

McCoy, who took his score to 101 – 35 clear of his closest championship pursuer Richard Johnson – when completing a double on Present Bleu's stablemate Turkestan, added: 'Last season I was off for five weeks early on with concussion. Then with the foot-and-mouth epidemic and the weather I missed riding 200 winners, which was a big disappointment as I want to do it two seasons running and keep getting it wrong.

'But this season has gone well, and I'm ahead of schedule to beat my best-ever score of 253 if the horses stay well.'

McCoy said he was 'going to pretend now that I'm back to scratch and starting again', as he pursues his second century, with 300 winners remaining a possibility.

He added: 'One of my goals is to win every race I'm eligible to ride in at the Festival, and there are still quite a few I've never won, including the Sun Alliance Chase and the Sun Alliance Hurdle, and also the National Hunt Handicap.

'I also obviously want to win a Grand National, and I was gutted by what happened to Blowing Wind last year. Something will have to be very impressive this season for me not to want to ride him again.'

McCoy has now ridden more than 1,400 winners in Britain and is on course to beat Richard Dunwoody's total career record of 1,699 victories.

Come December, racing was once again getting exercised as to why the rest of the world in general and the BBC Sports Personality of the Year awards in particular could not recognise the phenomenon we had in our midst. Alan Byrne, then editor of the Racing Post, *waded in.*

CLARE BALDING tells an instructive story about Tony McCoy at the BBC Sports Personality of the Year awards. It seems that as he observed a succession of Britain's heroic sporting failures after last year's event, many of whom had been lauded during the show itself, the inestimable McCoy could be heard asking repeatedly: 'What's he won, then?'

It will not come as a surprise to anyone in racing that McCoy should place such a high value on winning. It's just a pity that the

'Remember the advice offered in relation to elections in Ireland: "Vote early – and vote often."'

ALAN BYRNE

general sporting public hasn't learned to place as high a value on McCoy as it should. The man's talent is awe-inspiring.

The *Sun* has been running a commendable campaign on its racing pages to persuade readers to ring in and cast their vote for the champion jockey for the overall Sports Personality of the Year – a suggestion also made by our own Net Prophet column a fortnight ago.

It is to be hoped that as a result the best jump jockey ever might earn some hugely deserved wider recognition by making the shortlist for the Beckham-destined award.

But if he doesn't, it won't detract from McCoy's amazing achievements. Nor will it be any reflection on him. It will simply be a reminder of the job to be done in securing a wider audience for our sport – to the point perhaps where the Sun's back page and not its racing page might one day be spearheading the campaign.

In the meantime, remember the advice offered in relation to elections in Ireland prior to independence: 'Vote early – and vote often.'

The campaigns were once again 'not-in-the-first-six' fruitless. McCoy's best answer, as ever, was what he did on the track. Andrew King was on hand to witness the next milestone.

TONY McCOY yesterday reflected contentedly on the latest landmark in a heady career filled with achievements, but is not resting on his laurels after riding his 1,500th winner in Britain at Exeter.

The champion jockey immediately reiterated his desire to break the longest surviving record in his profession.

While he is closing in on the most career winners of a jump jockey, held by Richard Dunwoody, he has his eye firmly set on the 269 record of Sir Gordon Richards for the most winners in a season. McCoy has 103 racing days left this season to ride the 83 winners he needs to reach 270 for the campaign.

After completing the 1,500, McCoy said: 'It's obviously a great landmark but there's a few other things I'd like to do which are more important to me and that is to beat Richard Dunwoody's record and ride more winners than Sir Gordon Richards.

'The way things are going I've got a chance of breaking Sir Gordon's record this season as long as the weather is kind and there are not too many abandoned meetings, and if I stay sound and clear of suspensions.

'It's a long, long way away and for now I'll just keep riding as many winners as possible and doing my best for all the owners and trainers who keep supporting me.'

The champion completed a full circle in bagging win number 1,500 at Exeter.

McCoy said: 'It's great to put the 1,500 on the board at the track where I rode my first ever winner in Britain.

'That was on a horse called Chickabiddy just over seven years ago.'

The winners were now coming by the shedload but on 23 January 2002 came the most bizarre of them all. Our reporter Will O'Hanlon had probably been expecting a routine day ...

CHAOS REIGNED at Southwell yesterday as Tony McCoy gained what must go down as the most remarkable win of his career aboard Family Business.

Racegoers and punters in betting shops across Britain watched in amazement as, one by one, all seven runners in the Feast of St Raymond Novices' Chase fell, unseated or refused – some more than once – until there were no horses left running.

The prospect of a void race loomed but, almost inevitably, it was McCoy who seized the chance of victory. Even then the drama did not end, as the stewards held an inquiry into whether the result should stand.

The race was picked up by national television, and the non-racing public's viewing of such mayhem may have caused discomfort for racing's rulers.

*The Feast of St Raymond Novices'
Chase, Southwell, 23 January 2002:
how betting shop viewers saw AP
unseated from Family Business.*

Thankfully, all the horses returned unscathed, but Mark Bradburne, who fell from Oh No Whiskey, was taken to hospital for precautionary x-rays, which showed no cause for concern.

McCoy had been unseated from the Martin Pipe-trained odds-on favourite at the middle fence in the straight on the second circuit and was making his way back in disgust when he realised there was mayhem out on the course. He made a snap decision to remount.

The incident on the far side featured Red Radish, What A Wonder and Eaux Les Coeurs, all of whom departed at the fourth last. Red Radish refused, What A Wonder – who had earlier unseated rider Howard Ephgrave and been remounted – blundered and unseated again, and Eaux Les Coeurs (another who had also fallen and been remounted) also downed tools.

With Oh No Whiskey, Star Control and Joe Luke having already departed, there were now no runners standing – until McCoy spotted his chance to record win number 210 for the season.

Pipe's travelling head lad Bob Hodge said: 'We'd caught the horse on the far turn and were leading him back when we heard the commentator calling all the fallers on the far side, so Tony said, "I'm getting back on."'

Family Business, an 8-11 shot, then came home in his own time and McCoy received a great reception, with one racegoer shouting: 'You deserve a medal for that, Tony, but don't forget to weigh in.'

The champion, for his part, had mixed feelings. 'I felt embarrassed at first because, basically, I fell off,' he said. 'But I don't mind how I win in the end – I'd be happy to win another like that in half an hour.'

He added: 'It's unbelievable, I've never had one finish alone after being remounted. They'd gone too quick, but by the time they got tired I'd fallen off!'

Heavy overnight rain, which had caused the ground to change from a forecast 'good, good to firm in places', to 'good to soft', contributed to the mayhem, but Rupert Wakley, rider of Eaux Les Coeurs, did suggest the fences should be looked at. 'I just wonder if they should be a bit more inviting,' he said.

The action then switched to the stewards' room, where the issue was whether McCoy had blundered in taking Family Business back to the second last fence in the straight and jumping that fence again or whether he should have recommenced his journey after that fence.

An inquiry was held, advice was taken from Portman Square, and Family Business's victory was confirmed.

The stewards also fielded a query from a bookmakers' representative, rather bizarrely suggesting that the judge should have left his box before Family Business, who took more than ten and a half minutes, had time to complete. 'We disagreed with that view,' said Phil Tuck, the stipendiary steward. 'In fact, it was the judge's duty to do quite the opposite.'

And in the midst of it, as Seb Vance relayed, a couple of backers took the chance of a lifetime.

IT IS VIRTUALLY impossible for punters to get 1,000-1 about an odds-on shot, especially when Tony McCoy is riding, but yesterday two punters managed just that, each netting £2,000 in the process.

McCoy was unseated on the 8-11 favourite Family Business on the second circuit in the Feast of St Raymond Novices' Chase at

Southwell. However, on seeing the carnage unfolding ahead of him, he opted to remount and was the only finisher.

The two quick-thinking – if optimistic – punters placed their £2 bets on the website Betfair (the betting-exchange firm where bets are matched on a person-to-person basis), after seeing someone had offered to lay 1,000-1 about Family Business winning.

Mark Davies, director of communications for Betfair.com, explained how the sequence of events unfolded:

'McCoy was unseated and, while he was cursing his bad luck, one of our clients put Family Business up at 1,000-1.

'People lay at these prices because they think it's easy money.

'However, this layer says he was acting in a "community spirit", whereby you indicate to fellow punters that a horse has fallen by offering a maximum price to a minimum stake.'

The hapless layer, who wishes to remain anonymous, accepted his losses in good spirits.

'Under Betfair rules, I am happy for it to be honoured, but you can be sure I will not be alerting other users about fallers in the future, and Tony McCoy's off my Christmas card list as well!', the layer said.

Davies revealed that the price was the biggest that had been laid and won on Betfair, beating the 600-1 that a user had laid to a punter's £10 on Bolivia beating Brazil after they had gone a goal down in a World Cup qualifier.

Coral reported that one of their punters had staked a single bet of £5,000 on McCoy's mount, but had walked out of the shop in disgust and, as of last night, had not returned.

Any way of winning would do – and they were coming on the flood. Bruce Jackson was at Plumpton when another round number was achieved on 25 February 2002.

TONY McCOY reached another milestone when passing 250 winners in a season in record time with success on Going Global at Plumpton yesterday.

The champion needs four more winners to break his own record for a season, and is 20 short of eclipsing the British record of Sir Gordon Richards set on the Flat in 1947.

The win, from three rides, maintains his necessary winner-a-day strike rate to get to a magical 300 by the end of the season on 27 April.

Even McCoy is slightly taken aback with his relentless progress.

'I am ahead of where I expected to be – I thought I would do well to reach 250 by mid-March,' he said.

The last 50 winners have come in just 38 racing days. He topped 200 on 11 January and, if he maintains that rate, there is a chance of the record being achieved on the big stage at the Cheltenham Festival.

If anybody still needed convincing about McCoy's unquenchable desire to win, he produced another example even in defeat when persuading the wandering and reluctant Ambry to snatch second

The fastest 250: AP and Going Global join Eaux Les Coeurs – who is about to slip and fall – at the second last.

in the final race, when fourth looked the best he could achieve around the home turn.

No wonder trainer Gary Moore said: 'Tony is the best ever. I always look to use him and hope I can help him to the record with a few more winners.'

Even when records are tumbling, disaster still lurks. It came on Valiramix in the 2002 Champion Hurdle. A week earlier at Wincanton, AP had told me that this was his best ride of the Festival. When triple winner Istabraq pulled up hopelessly out of sorts after jumping just two hurdles you could see what AP had meant. Even more so when he cruised effortlessly into the lead three out. Then a leg snapped – and what had been a soaring racehorse became no more than a sack of meat. For McCoy it ruined everything.

As the Festival ended, AP spoke to Jon Lees.

A MISERABLE Cheltenham Festival for Tony McCoy could not be salvaged by a win in the penultimate race of the three-day meeting.

The champion jockey, in tears when Valiramix had to be put down after breaking his shoulder in the Smurfit Champion Hurdle, was barely cheered by the success of Royal Auclair in the Cathcart Chase.

McCoy had begun the meeting with an outstanding book of rides, yet failed to finish in either the Champion Hurdle or the Tote Cheltenham Gold Cup, and was only fourth on defending champion Edredon Bleu in the Queen Mother Champion Chase.

To make matters worse he had missed two other Martin Pipe-trained winners because he was on board better-fancied stablemates.

McCoy said afterwards: 'I'm pleased I've had a winner but this doesn't bring Valiramix back, nothing will be consolation for losing him.

'I was in bed by 9pm on Tuesday night but couldn't get to sleep until 1am. I am better off on my own then, at least that way nobody comes to try to cheer me up. It's just one of those things.'

McCoy acknowledged the applause from a crowd fully conscious of his earlier disappointments after his victory on Royal Auclair.

Pipe said: 'Everyone was cheering on AP, which was great. All the punters were on and it was a good result for a five-year-old.'

McCoy is at Chepstow today with seven rides, and is seven wins short of the 270 he needs to beat the British record held by Sir Gordon Richards.

Not all press coverage had been as understanding. Some even called him a 'miserable git'. He didn't think it fair, and on 16 March 2002 we reported:

TONY McCOY yesterday put the record straight on his miserable Cheltenham Festival and hit back at all those who had labelled him a bad loser.

The champion jockey looked in a distraught state throughout the three-day meeting. However, he insisted yesterday that his Cheltenham anguish had nothing to do with his tally of five seconds and just one winner, but everything to do with the death of his Champion Hurdle mount, the towering grey Valiramix.

McCoy said: 'I'm all right now, but I was reading in some papers this morning that I was not happy because I had a lot of seconds at the Festival – it wasn't anything to do with finishing second on a few.

'It was the grey horse's death that really upset me. It wasn't getting beaten, it was losing possibly the best horse we've had for a long time. It's annoying finishing second and I hate it, but it was Valiramix that upset me.

'I know I'm not sometimes the most pleasant person in the world, but a lot of people got it wrong in saying I was upset because I kept finishing second.'

McCoy suffered a similar ordeal at the 2000 Festival, when Gold Cup mount Gloria Victis had to be destroyed after breaking a leg.

'It was actually a harder week for me than when we lost Gloria Victis two years ago,' McCoy said. 'That happened on the Thursday in the Gold Cup and people didn't really see how that affected me – no-one had to look at me to see how much I was hurt.

The Valiramix disaster proved but a temporary setback. True, the winner flow dried exasperatingly for a while, but come 3 April 2002, one of the biggest records of all went the way of the rest. Rodney Masters was at Warwick to chronicle the moment.

TONY McCOY finally made history yesterday as he ended his agonising wait to beat Sir Gordon Richards' 55-year-old all-time record of 269 for the number of winners in a season – and immediately promised his vast army of followers there will be no easing off in his relentless pursuit of success.

This most modest of champions also confessed he was embarrassed to be compared with Richards after beating his total on Martin Pipe's novice hurdler Valfonic in front of a cheering crowd at Warwick. He was completing a 78-1 treble, having won earlier on Robin Dickin's Shampooed and Charlie Morlock's Shepherds Rest.

'This will take some while to sink in, but I wouldn't dream of comparing myself with someone like Sir Gordon,' he said. 'Sure

I've ridden 270 winners, but he was champion 26 times and he's definitely got me beaten on that one – I can't see me going on until I'm nearly 50!'

Richards would certainly have been proud to claim the ride on Valfonic as one of his own. McCoy held up this doubtful stayer in last position before making his move down the back straight. Landing flat-footed two flights out failed to break his charge and he won by one and a quarter lengths.

McCoy's dedication and never-say-die spirit are his trademarks, adored by punters and admired by his fellow professionals. He pledged there would be no change in his approach to the job.

'The championship is very important to me and I'll be doing my best to hang on to it for as long as possible. This record will not last for ever. Someone better than me will come along some time soon to beat it, that's for certain. Records are made to be broken.

'I've been very fortunate to go through the season without injury. I need only look at what has happened to [the injured] Adrian Maguire and Joe Tizzard to be reminded of that.'

'Records are made to be broken' – and AP celebrates his 270th winner.

McCoy also pointed out that he was operating from a privileged position, and diverted credit in every direction, including to Billy Rock, with whom he started riding out as a schoolboy in Northern Ireland, Jim Bolger, Toby Balding and Pipe.

'I've a terrific team who make the job so much easier for me,' he added. 'There's Dave Roberts, who knows the form book inside out and books my rides, and Gee Armytage, who takes all the pressure off at home by organising me superbly. I've also a driver, and then there's Mr Pipe.

'If you look at the facts, no jockey has an easier life than me. Unlike most of the boys, I don't have to troop up and down the country riding out for various trainers.'

McCoy was not predicting whether 300 winners will be within his range, with just three weeks remaining of the current season.

'Before even thinking about that I want to concentrate on Aintree and the Grand National,' he said. 'I suppose some people may regard me as a failure unless I win a National – I may even do so myself.

'The 300 will not be easy because I have to serve a two-day ban next week, but I'll be doing my best.'

To reflect on an historic moment, enter the Racing Post's *resident historian John Randall.*

IN AN AGE OF HYPE, when anything half a per cent above average is routinely described as great, it is hard to do justice to Tony McCoy's awesome new record.

Sir Gordon Richards was statistically the greatest British jockey of all time and, in beating his tally of 269 wins in the 1947 Flat season, McCoy has broken a record which seemed beyond the reach of mere mortals.

It is true that in 1947 the Flat season lasted only eight months, whereas it has taken McCoy 11 months, and more rides than Richards, to set the new standard.

Yet in view of the extra distance ridden by jump jockeys, and the greater hazards they face, no-one can legitimately claim that McCoy's achievement is inferior to that of Richards.

In any case, Richards had more winning opportunities than Fred Archer when he was breaking the latter's records, and no one called his feats bogus.

Some of Richards' records will never be beaten. No other jockey will be champion 26 times, win 4,870 races in a career or score 12 double-centuries in Britain.

His 1947 seasonal record also looked invulnerable for many years, but the advent of 12-month seasons changed matters. Frankie Dettori threatened it for most of 1994, though he eventually had to settle for a score of 233.

Even then it looked impossible for a jump jockey to approach the record, but the introduction of summer jumping in 1995 and the emergence of a statistical phenomenon in McCoy finally put it within reach.

There is no reason why his feat should not be compared with that of Richards just because they operated in different branches of the sport. After all, Henry Cecil held the equivalent trainers' record with 180 wins in 1987 until Martin Pipe beat it with 208 victories in 1988-89. What matters is the overall record; it is irrelevant whether it is set on the Flat or over jumps.

Gordon Richards dominated the British Turf for many years through his achievements and his personality. A miner's son who became the only jockey to be knighted, he was racing's most cherished hero and even now some people get upset at anything which diminishes his stature – like his records being broken.

They need not worry. This particular record has a worthy new owner – one who may, on his eventual retirement, occupy a place in the jumps pantheon similar to that of Richards on the Flat.

The one place McCoy still could not occupy was the Grand National winner's circle, and 2002 offered no relief when favourite Blowing Wind, third in 2001, could finish only third again. But the golden run of 2001-02 had a suitably golden conclusion with a new European

COMPARISONS

SIR GORDON RICHARDS

wins:	269
rides:	835
strike rate:	32.2%

TONY McCOY

wins:	270
rides:	932
strike rate:	29.0%

'Richards was very like McCoy – his determination to win outreached every other jockey. I've nothing but admiration for them both – they would have been good generals in a war.'

JIMMY LINDLEY,
who rode against Gordon Richards in the early 1950s

McCOY'S SEASON 2001-2002	
wins:	289
rides:	1006
strike rate:	29%
position in championship:	1st

record 289th winner of the campaign. Jon Lees saw the curtain fall at Sandown Park.

TONY McCOY, whose failure to identify the best Martin Pipe contender cost him an occasional big-race winner during the season, had no such problems in the Attheraces Gold Cup at Sandown on Saturday, when he rounded off a record-breaking campaign in style.

McCoy celebrated his crowning as champion jump jockey for the seventh consecutive time by claiming his first success in the race formerly run as the Whitbread, bringing him a final score for the 2001-02 season of 289.

A week earlier McCoy had overlooked subsequent Scottish Grand National winner Take Control in favour of Cyfor Malta, whom he pulled up.

This time he picked correctly, selecting Bounce Back from a pool of six and steering the horse to secure a famous one-two for the Pipe yard as he beat Dark Stranger by eight lengths.

Attheraces Gold Cup, Sandown Park, 27 April 2002: AP and Bounce Back clear at the last.

Bounce Back, who joined Pipe for a reported £250,000 last summer, had since proved a costly horse to follow, winning only once from seven starts, despite outings over both hurdles and fences.

But the six-year-old found the step up to an extreme distance much more to his liking as he delivered the first significant racing success for owner Belinda Harvey. He now shares with 1958 winner Taxidermist the honour of being the race's youngest winner.

McCoy said: 'I went through all the horses we were running. He was still unexposed as a chaser. He'd been a bit disappointing, but he was the one I knew had lots of ability and the potential to win a big race.

'He'd run over hurdles lately and I thought the switch to fences might bring out the best in him. I thought he was capable of winning a race like this and he jumped better than he's ever done.

'I suppose at least today he has repaid us a bit. He's disappointed me a little but I'm pleased with him now.'

McCoy was able to ride the kind of waiting race most expected from Frenchman's Creek but, while the 11-4 favourite came under pressure from the final bend, the champion was still travelling comfortably on Bounce Back and, once they had collared the pace-setting Dark Stranger at the last, he was pushed clear to victory.

Frenchman's Creek battled on to claim third, with last year's winner Ad Hoc fourth.

McCoy added: 'I was hoping something would take me to Dark Stranger down the back. I'm always very wary of letting a Pipe horse get too far away from me – they keep going.'

Pipe said: 'Tony gave him a peach of a ride. He was jumping from fence to fence.'

The end of that season might have been sublime; the start of the new one, 2002-03, was nothing if not ridiculous.

The very first day saw the champion and six other riders given a hefty seven-day suspension for apparently going the wrong side of a false running rail. Amidst much official blushing, the subsequent inquiry found the fault lay entirely with the racecourse, and the fines were quashed.

Not all summer appearances were so controversial.

CHAMPION JUMP JOCKEY Tony McCoy received an honorary doctorate from Queen's University in Belfast on Wednesday. The degree is doctor of the university and is for services to sport.

James O'Kane, registrar of the university, described McCoy in the citation as 'a meteor which flashes across the sporting firmament only once in a lifetime or perhaps once in a century.'

He added: 'I am sure you will agree that Tony McCoy has everything – commitment, courage, skill in abundance and remarkable dedication.

'He is an outstanding ambassador for his profession, as well as for Northern Ireland.'

A delighted McCoy said: 'The only regret I have is that Billy Rock, the trainer who launched my career, can't be here at the ceremony as he is on holiday in Crete.'

Time was when jump jockeys and trainers took summer holidays too. But that was before Pipe and McCoy rewrote the record books. Colin Russell saw a memorable day at Market Rasen on 20 July 2002.

EVEN BY THEIR OWN extraordinary standards Saturday was a remarkable day for Martin Pipe and Tony McCoy. Not only did they win the two feature events with Puntal and Chicuelo, but Pipe went on to complete a four-timer – worth a total of £67,351 – and seal 'a great week' to beat his own record for the fastest 50 wins in a season.

McCoy, who rode the quartet, also won the juvenile hurdle to make it five winners from six rides.

In fact McCoy, after five wins from five rides, had the anoraks scurrying to scour the record books to confirm that no jump jockey had ever won six races from six rides on one card. The research,

Tote Scoop6 Summer Plate, Market Rasen, 20 July 2002: Chicuelo (left) heads Star Jack at the last.

though, was unnecessary, as the champion fell three out on his final mount, though he remounted to finish second.

However, with these five winners McCoy's career total is now 1,676, which puts him only two behind Peter Scudamore in the all-time list of winningmost jump jockeys and only 23 behind the most successful rider ever, Richard Dunwoody.

The Scudamore record fell on 28 July 2002 when Polar Champ won a novice chase at Newton Abbot. Dunwoody's total was just a month away. On 27 August 2002, Will O'Hanlon saw the hand of history tap AP McCoy on the shoulder yet again.

TONY McCOY has scaled many a peak in his astonishing career, but victory on Mighty Montefalco at Uttoxeter yesterday took him to the pinnacle of the jumping firmament, as he overhauled Richard Dunwoody to become the most successful jump jockey in the world.

Victory in the Everedge Handicap Hurdle allowed McCoy to reach the magical figure of 1,700 career wins, breaking his fellow Ulsterman Dunwoody's record, which had stood for just three years.

When Dunwoody retired, it had seemed a record that would take a lot of beating, but so relentless has McCoy's pursuit been in those three seasons, that the champion has passed it while still in his prime, with the prospect of setting a final mark of his own which is unlikely ever to be matched.

McCoy had arrived at Uttoxeter needing two wins to reach his goal. He did not waste time. Win number 1,699 was slotted home when Dream With Me landed the opening novice hurdle with the minimum of fuss, the 1-3 shot coasting home by nine lengths.

One small step – but a giant leap in the annals of racing history – later and the summit had been reached, as McCoy steered 8-13 shot Mighty Montefalco, trained by Jonjo O'Neill, to a hard-earned victory over My Good Son.

Uttoxeter, 28 July 2002: AP's agent Dave Roberts greets the winningmost jump jockey of all time.

The 28-year-old champion returned to a rousing reception, and a beaming O'Neill was the first to offer his congratulations as the new record-holder dismounted.

O'Neill, himself prominent in the all-time jockeys' list, said: 'He's one in a million. I can't think of a fault he's got – and he's such a nice lad to work with. What he's done in eight years is unbelievable, and it's nice that he's been able to get the record on one of mine.'

Peter S. Thompson, owner of Mighty Montefalco, who spends half his time in Maryland and the rest in London, said: 'It's terrific and I've been dreaming about this.'

McCoy's own response to beating Dunwoody's mark showed just how much he rates the former great.

'I'm over the moon to have done it,' he said. 'Richard was my idea of the perfect jockey, and a true professional with it. It's a tremendous feeling to have passed him.

'It's also special in that Richard was my boyhood hero when I was growing up in Northern Ireland.

'I know how lucky I am in the people I work for and in my agent [Dave Roberts],' he continued. 'You could say I'm a very spoiled jockey, but there are still plenty of things I haven't achieved – I haven't won a Grand National or a King George yet – and I shall keep going as long as there are targets to be achieved and I enjoy the job.

'I'm sure there will always be someone who comes along in the future who is better than me, and before I retire I want to make sure I ride as many winners as possible, so I make his job of beating my total as difficult as possible.'

Victory number 1,700 came on McCoy's 6,336th ride in Britain – compared to Dunwoody's tally of more than 9,300 – and put him on the 97 mark for the season.

At the same stage last season, when he broke Sir Gordon Richards's 54-year-old British record for wins in a season and ended with 289 wins, he had ridden 87 winners. Paddy Power issued odds of 3-1 for McCoy to reach 300 for the season.

'It's phenomenal what he has achieved. I don't think anyone has ever achieved so much in any other sport. It really is amazing what he has done in such a short time. His dedication to the sport is tremendous and again one doesn't realise how he has to struggle with his weight. His whole life is devoted to riding horses, and horses run for him, as we saw with his 1,700th winner.'

MARTIN PIPE

'Even when I won my first championship title I didn't think for
one moment I'd beat Richard's record,' said McCoy.

'All I want to do in life is ride winners. I'm fortunate that I'm in
the best possible position to do just that. Let's face it, if you found
the worst jockey in the world and put him up on one of Martin
Pipe's, it would still win.

'I keep in touch with Richard more than most do in the weighing
room, and we're good friends. I've no doubt he was the best jump
jockey I rode against. He had everything, and in my eyes his riding
was perfection.

'While mentioning the great jump jockeys of this generation,
I'd also have to include Adrian Maguire and Charlie Swan. When
youngsters ask me who they should watch to learn most about
jockeyship in general, I point them towards Michael Kinane
because he has no flaw.

'I've been incredibly fortunate that throughout my career I've had the right people advising me. There was Billy Rock, Jim Bolger, Toby Balding and now Martin Pipe.

'Jim took great care to mould my character, to make sure I not only rode properly, but spoke properly and conducted myself in the right manner.

'People keep asking what's my next target, and the answer is simple enough. Winning on the next horse I ride.

'I've not organised a celebration. I might just have an early night, though I suspect the lads might have something else in mind.'

McCoy was now into uncharted territory, and looking back on 2002, it is truly astonishing to think that he had a whole new and triumphantly successful phase of his career ahead.

'He's simply as complete a jockey as there's been, and to think that he's already broken Richard's record when he's still in his twenties shows what a phenomenon he is.'

CARL LLEWELLYN

SUPREMACY

Into September 2002 and the McCoy bandwagon was once again rolling, and with ever increasing speed. On 5 September the Racing Post *was reporting from Newton Abbot on yet another fastest century of wins (13 ahead of the previous season's record-breaking schedule) but two items from Rodney Masters' golden pen over the next week reminded us that McCoy was a human being as well as a jockey …*

TONY McCOY retold the story about the first time he rode at Stratford, a few days after he came over from Northern Ireland. He didn't have a pair of boots that fitted, so a kindly valet took pity on the lad and sorted him out with the right-sized footwear without a fuss.

'The valet warned me those particular boots would take plenty of filling,' recalled McCoy, 'because they belonged to Peter Scudamore.'

Yesterday, McCoy and other past and present stars from the weighing room gathered to honour that recently retired valet, John Buckingham, known to them all as 'Buck'.

It was a gesture of sincere thanks from the sportsmen to Buckingham for his tireless endeavours in the organisation of similar golf days at his local club, Cherwell, near Banbury in Oxfordshire, which have raised more than £54,000 for the Injured Jockeys' Fund.

'Everyone admires and respects Buck, and this was a great idea to thank him for his efforts over the years,' added McCoy.

A measure of the respect in which Buckingham is held can be gauged from the fact that the likes of Richard Dunwoody and Graham McCourt were among the 150 or so who turned out for the event, and they weren't even playing.

Buckingham, 62, sold his valeting business when Tom, his brother and partner, died. He had 'nannied' all of jump racing's modern-day champions, including McCoy, John Francome, Dunwoody and Scudamore.

In retirement, life has been far from easy. He was recently diagnosed with diabetes and underwent surgery on his spine to fix a painful legacy from his days as a jockey.

Newton Abbot, 4 September 2002: the fastest century of winners, courtesy of Toi Express.

Previous spread: Cheltenham, 16 March 2004: AP and Well Chief win the Irish Independent Arkle Trophy from Kicking King (Barry Geraghty).

However, old friendships have not died and a week doesn't go by without Francome telephoning to check on his progress.

Also playing yesterday was Josh Gifford, and that brought back memories of the day the Buckingham-ridden Foinavon beat the Gifford-ridden Honey End in the 1967 Grand National.

'Rarely a day passes without someone mentioning Foinavon to me,' said Buckingham. 'Josh always reminds me that I was lucky because my horse was the only one to get over the fence first time in that pile-up. In turn, I remind Josh that my horse would have won anyway.'

More than £5,000 was raised for the testimonial yesterday, which included an auction in the evening. The event was organised by Buckingham's long-time pals Bill Pigott and Malcolm Bachelor.

Rodney's next dispatch was published on 12 September 2002, but to understand it immediately you need to appreciate that it was written on the day before – that is, exactly one year on from the Twin Towers catastrophe that was 9/11.

TONY McCOY recalled he was on the golf course at the time with John Francome and Mick Fitzgerald. His mobile telephone rang. His mother Claire broke the news.

McCoy was aware that Cantor Fitzgerald, a company within which he had forged close friendships through their racing sponsorships, occupied several floors close to the top of the World Trade Center towers.

Religion and racing aren't always the most intimate of bedfellows but yesterday, as the Reverend Mike Vockins stressed that the world was desperately in need of peace and understanding, you could see jumping's champion nod in approval.

At 1.46pm, as he and the rest of us stood in silence at Hereford, the contrast of the venue was as striking as the solidarity.

Manhattan, population 1.5 million, the frenzied financial hub of the United States. Hereford, population 51,000, home of a treasured medieval map of the world, the *Mappa Mundi*, of timber-framed houses and Strongbow.

Lining up.

'This was the time to give something back.'

TONY McCOY

With summer throwing a final fling, this timeless patch of rural England was at its glorious best. A soft breeze drifting in from the Black Mountains, the programme of fund-raising events played out under a pale blue sky. As many were to remark, a similar tint to the sky as had been over New York on that morning twelve months ago. The last morning for 658 members of Cantor's staff.

Religion can be guilty of overplaying, even stifling, these occasions, but the Rev. Vockins got the balance right in his short prayers conducted from the paddock.

You'd expect nothing less from a man who clearly understands sport and sportsmen. Over many decades he was secretary to Worcestershire County Cricket Club, and also served in the same capacity to England under-21 touring teams.

McCoy had been mulling over for some time how racing could best assist the families of the Cantor employees who'd lost their lives. 'Cantor have been very good to racing, and very helpful to me in the two years I've been sponsored by them,' he said. 'This was the time to give something back.'

He donated riding fees and prize-money from his four winners – which totted up to around £1,500 – to the relief fund.

Items he donated to either the raffle or auction included the framed breeches he'd worn 15 days earlier at Uttoxeter when breaking Richard Dunwoody's all-time record of winners.

McCoy was in no need of them yesterday, anyway. He and the other two Cantor-sponsored jockeys, Mick Fitzgerald and Carl Llewellyn, wore black breeches.

Racing's wounded soldiers turned up to support the cause. Richard Johnson, stitches removed from his broken leg, is already back in the swimming pool rebuilding muscle, and champion conditional Henry Oliver is more advanced in his recovery from a similar injury.

Mid-afternoon, two helicopters dropped in, depositing Zara Phillips and her teammates from Britain's young riders' eventing squad. Evidently they were unable to come earlier, or by conventional transport, because they'd been busy holding a bonding session in preparation for the European championships, imminent in Austria.

Phillips was due to make her racecourse debut in the charity race – incidentally, a fifth win of the day for McCoy on the Ian Balding-trained Memorial Arch – but she was a late defection, perhaps anxious to convince her eventing chums that her attention was fully focused on their sport.

Her appearance in the saddle yesterday would have no doubt boosted the crowd, but organisers were pleased enough with a crowd well up for a normal midweek fixture.

Top lot at the auction was £7,000 from owner Bernard Gover for a box on the second day of Royal Ascot. Other money-raisers included £2,500 for a nomination to Celtic Swing, donated by Peter Savill. In all, the day raised around £25,000.

Humour, thank the Lord, is never far removed from this sport, and yesterday's event, solemn as it was, had its share. As Olympic heavyweight champion Audley Harrison stepped into a full-size ring for an after-racing exhibition sparring session that lasted an hour, a chuckle went up when one local accent remarked: 'Audley's standing in for George Duffield. He couldn't make it in time from Doncaster.'

Audley Harrison would eat more in one meal than McCoy would in a week – especially when a big race looms up.

TONY McCOY has committed himself to a daily diet of vitamin pills, a piece of chicken and a Jaffa Cake as he tries to shed vital pounds for his ride on red-hot Thomas Pink Gold Cup favourite Chicuelo.

With the Martin Pipe-trained hope set to carry either 10st or 10st 1lb in Saturday's Cheltenham feature, McCoy has taken on the most meagre of menus in an attempt to ensure the ever shortening market leader carries no excess weight.

McCoy, who rode at 10st 2lb at Chepstow on Saturday before quickly 'ballooning' back to 10st 6lb, has not starved himself to a riding weight of 10st 1lb since February 2001.

He said: 'The important thing is that you have to keep your strength up. I'll keep eating little bits but I'll also be sweating an awful lot. I'll have hot baths morning and night and, although I won't be eating a lot, I'll be drinking lots of hot, sweet tea.'

Outlining his stark daily routine in the run-up to Saturday's £100,000 chase, the champion jockey said: 'I'll walk for an hour in the morning and, although I won't have breakfast, I will have a bit of chicken when I get to the races. After I get back home I'll have another cup of tea and a Jaffa Cake and then another sweat.

'On top of all that, I'll also be drinking plenty of mineral water and having lots of vitamin tablets – I don't really believe in them but I suppose there's got to be some sense in it!

'I've already been dieting for a week and I don't feel bad at all. I would crack up, though, if I had to do this sort of thing 52 weeks a year.'

If ever a horse failed in his side of the bargain, it was Chicuelo in the Thomas Pink. The further he went, the worse he jumped – and one particular blunder at the eighth fence forced the champion into the bumping ignominy of losing a stirrup iron.

But AP's continued high profile, and the publication of a well-received second autobiography, meant that his record-breaking exploits in the spring were not forgotten when the awards season came round in December.

TONY McCOY put a broad smile back on the face of British racing after he saw off the world heavyweight boxing champion and the England rugby union team's star kicker to finish third in the poll for BBC Sports Personality of the Year 2002.

While the seven-time champion would not be a living legend if even occasionally settling for anything less than first place, this latest tribute to McCoy's phenomenal talents provided a major fillip for the sport when it was urgently needed.

Racing has suffered a series of PR disasters since the summer, with the BBC programmes *Kenyon Confronts* and *Panorama* being

followed by the long-term bans imposed on Dermot Browne and Graham Bradley.

However, Britain's winningmost jump jockey, who loves rewriting the record books, excelled himself by coming to the rescue of the sport's battered image.

Looking back on Sunday night's star-studded event, McCoy said: 'It was brilliant. I am not normally happy with finishing third, but I suppose on this occasion I will make a huge exception, and hopefully people will think it is good for racing.'

BBC TV's Sports Review of the Year had a viewing audience estimated at 9 million as the Ulsterman, to prolonged applause, stepped up to be presented with his award at the climax of the programme.

He received 87,972 telephone votes to make the top three ahead of Lennox Lewis and Jonny Wilkinson.

Nobody from racing has ever lifted the prestigious trophy – captured this time by athlete Paula Radcliffe, with David Beckham runner-up – but McCoy, who only narrowly failed to make the shortlist of nominations twelve months ago, rose above recent controversies to equal the feat of Frankie Dettori.

The Italian was previously the best-placed jockey, having filled third spot following his 'Magnificent Seven' in 1996.

Even the housewives' favourite, Lester Piggott, never managed better than fourth, while Bob Champion, whose 1981 Aintree victory on Aldaniti was later celebrated in a film, had to be content with the team prize – as did Piggott, Vincent O'Brien and Nijinsky in 1970.

Eight years, eight championships and countless new records on, that third place is still the closest that AP has come in the BBC poll. Contrast that with Ireland, where Barry Geraghty was actually to win the equivalent in 2003. But the best contrast of all

'Mind-blowing': AP forces Iris's Gift (no. 1) past Ruby Walsh and Ad Hoc to win the Tripleprint Novices' Hurdle at Cheltenham, 14 December 2002.

was happening on the track, where Ruby was emerging as a true challenger to the supremacy of McCoy, as these Cheltenham thoughts from Alastair Down so vividly explain. (The 'Mr Talkalot' reference in the first paragraph can be explained by Alastair having broadcast alongside Ruby's brilliant if not exactly tongue-tied father Ted Walsh that afternoon.)

... BUT THE LASTING JOY of this day lay in the twin hands of AP McCoy and son of Mr Talkalot, Ruby Walsh.

In the gathering gloom of Saturday, as they ran the final race over three miles, we saw a mind-blowing celebration of the one thing that is fresh and new about this season – that there is at last a proper threat to the pre-eminence of McCoy.

As Ad Hoc and Ruby ran down to the last with AP and Iris's Gift hard on their case, the exchanges were going 10-1 against the champion.

But halfway up the run-in, there came over AP one of those seismic mind-and-body changes that makes the man half-frightening. Nobody knows more than Tony that there is now somebody else on the scene who truly punches his weight and all those mad genes and half-crazy instincts could be seen crying out, 'One day, you bastard, but not yet!' as he gouged Iris's Gift up past Walsh and Ad Hoc in the last 30 yards.

It's a long time since I have seen AP so happy with a result or so satisfied.

He has become the shining light of this sport. But the fact that Ruby is well up to his weight has added a new and hugely enjoyable dimension. I don't doubt the pair have their failings, but in a way that puts a spring in the step of this tired old man and I relish the full-cry clash over the years to come.

Safe home to both of you. You are going to take us all to places we have not been before, but it is vital you survive the journey.

Alastair's piece has proved a prophetic one as the continued McCoy-Walsh rivalry has become one of all sport's – not just racing's – greatest attractions.

But come Kempton on Boxing Day 2002, AP was once again waving the banner on his own. That was the day he clocked up a double century no fewer than 16 days quicker than the record-breaking schedule of the previous season. It was also the day when he righted a previous wrong with Gold Cup winner Best Mate.

In the 2001 King George VI Chase, AP had been criticised by some for being too cautious in his tactics before failing to catch the trail-blazing Florida Pearl. Mistake or not, and McCoy affirmed he was nursing Best Mate's then unproven stamina, it was gloriously rectified in 2002.

Cue this cerebral appreciation from the ever thoughtful James Willoughby.

TONY McCOY is not only one of the strongest and fittest jump jockeys ever, but once again proved himself a fantastic judge of pace in the Pertemps King George VI Chase at Kempton.

After winning the Boxing Day feature on Best Mate, he pointed out that he had ridden the winner more forcefully than ideal in order to execute a race-winning move. The split times proved both the veracity of this statement and showed the importance of the champion's tactics in shaping the outcome of a closely fought finish.

The middle section of the King George was run at virtually two-mile pace after a steady beginning. The field reached the sixth fence in nearly the same time as the earlier Feltham Novices' Chase won by Jair du Cochet. From that point, the tempo stepped up to such an extent that the King George field was 5.4 seconds faster to the 12th and 8.2 seconds faster to the 15th.

Approaching the fourth last fence, however, the gap began to close. The novices were just 4.2 seconds behind three out, and such was the zest with which tip-top novice Jair du Cochet came home, there was nearly parity between the two races at the line.

McCoy kicked the smooth-travelling Best Mate into the lead at the 15th fence – the hottest part of the race – rather than sitting still and allowing his less pacy opponents, notably the early

Opposite: Pertemps King George VI Chase, 26 December 2002: Best Mate and AP (stripes) beats Marlborough (Timmy Murphy).

leader Bacchanal, to stay in contention. This strategy forced some opponents to the point of exhaustion. Gaining a precious advantage stood Best Mate in good stead during the ensuing slog for home, because every length gained in the country was worth two in the closing stages on such cloying ground.

Best Mate proved he has guts as well as class and is clearly the one to beat in the Cheltenham Gold Cup. But he was well ridden for this narrow win over Marlborough, and again when winning last year's Blue Riband from Commanche Court.

Given the vagaries of a three-and-a-quarter-mile chase round Cheltenham, anybody who considers him already past the post in March is living in a world of make-believe.

Reading that article – indeed reading this book – it would be easy to think that McCoy was all but infallible in the saddle. It is not a line he takes: even the shortest of conversations tends to be laden with self-mocking groans at his own incompetence. But what happened when he lost his iron and fell straight off odds-on favourite Vanormix after the last flight at Cheltenham on New Year's Day 2003 was still something of a collector's item.

Most writers were too polite to say much more than a version of 'Homer nods', but Peter Thomas couldn't resist asking a proper question.

TODAY WE WILL put under the microscope that breed known as The Untouchables. Not Sean Connery, Andy Garcia and the little geeky one who brought Al Capone to book in the gritty gangster flick; not the Indians who, by some accident of birth, get the shortest possible shrift from their fellow men; and certainly not those folk who have a bath once a month whether they need it or not.

No, what we are talking about is the elite group who, by dint of their magnificent achievements and consequent lofty reputations, become immune from criticism from any quarter. Any who dare to question their infallibility and superhumanity are likely to be cast out of the herd and condemned to a protracted and lonely death on the fringes.

Few are called to join this lofty brigade. Sadly, most of those who are elevated get their call-up papers only at the point of death, thus being deprived of the benefits of immortality until such time as they can no longer enjoy them.

Jimi Hendrix is never disputed as the greatest guitarist ever to walk this earth. Whereas Clapton lost his edge and veered towards the middle of the road as a result of remaining alive, Hendrix, through a cruel-but-kind cocktail of youthful virtuosity and choking on his own vomit, moved on to join the multi-platinum supergroup in the sky.

Likewise Bobby Moore, who in life was unfairly remembered by many as the bloke who cost England qualification to the 1974 World Cup with that hideous gaffe against the Poles, but who, once he sadly popped his clogs, became unassailable at the pinnacle of British defenderdom, recalled only in terms of affection, respect and swapping shirts with Pele.

To achieve Untouchability during life, however, is a different matter entirely. But it seems as if Tony McCoy has done just that.

This became apparent on New Year's Day, and in its aftermath, following the ignominious departure of our mighty champion jockey from the saddle of Vanormix in the 2.15 at Cheltenham.

We've all seen the video a thousand times by now, so suffice it to say that AP disappeared out of the side door when about to launch his trademark late thrust on a horse that, while possibly beaten at the time, was by no means a lost cause, particularly for those who had backed him down to 4-5.

From the comfort of my armchair, I watched open-mouthed as the unthinkable occurred, and then waited for the replay to confirm my suspicions that either (a) McCoy's saddle had slipped, (b) his stirrup iron had broken or (c) Norman Williamson had tried to put him over the rail. When the pictures revealed a simple human error, my gob had never been so smacked.

'When the pictures revealed a simple human error, my gob had never been so smacked.'

PETER THOMAS

The Channel 4 team was similarly taken aback. 'Just one of those things' was the harshest criticism from them, along with mitigation about wetness, slipperiness and prevailing wind direction. The following day's press coverage confirmed this leniency.

My mind wandered in the direction of Thierry Doumen. What, I asked myself, would have been the reaction had it been the Gallic whipping boy in – or rather out of – the saddle on this sorry occasion, rather than the Untouchable McCoy?

Doumen (not my favourite jockey by any means) had been roundly rogered by the British hacks for winning a farcically slowly run race in heavy going at Ascot on Baracouda, on the basis that they thought he should have won it more easily, instead of almost allowing McCoy to nick it from the front on an inferior animal. Perhaps so, but undoubtedly if McCoy had given Baracouda the same ride, he would have been lauded for his masterful judgement of pace in atrocious conditions.

In similar vein, I doubt there's an armchair punter in the land who believes that if Doumen had been the man who fell to earth at Cheltenham, he would have been afforded the same sympathetic reception as McCoy by racegoers and pencil-squeezers alike.

Can you imagine reading: 'In an unfortunate incident yesterday, the luckless Thierry Doumen, through no fault of his own, forfeited a winning chance on an odds-on favourite when, because of the wrong kind of rain on his stirrups, he completely forgivably fell off'? Which was pretty much what was said about McCoy.

No, it would have been: 'In another display of onion-carrying ineptitude, despicable Daddy's-boy foreigner Thierry Doumen cost good old British punters hundreds of thousands of pounds as he flopped from Vanormix like a sack of spuds when on the brink of almost certain victory. Luckily, having remounted, he was dragged from his horse by irate spectators and beaten to death with a ham and cheese baguette.'

This is not to say that Doumen is within an English Channel's width of McCoy as a rider, but surely we can bring ourselves to roast the great man now and then – if only for the novelty value.

Rehearsing with Foster and Allen at The Blowing Stone Inn in Lambourn before recording 'The Fields of Athenry' in aid of the Injured Jockeys' Fund, January 2003. Left to right: John Kavanagh, Adrian Maguire, Seamus Durack, AP McCoy, Mick Fitzgerald, Jimmy McCarthy, Timmy Murphy and Eddie Ahern.

In early 2003 the Racing Post *ran a poll amongst its readers to find the greatest personality of racing history. It was won by the unique training genius that was Vincent O'Brien – but not before there had been some magnificent citations on behalf of other heroes. This time Peter Thomas didn't stint the praise.*

THE WORST KIND of 'Best of All Time' lists are those compiled by or voted for by uninformed people with the attention spans of mayflies. The No. 1 is so certain to have been plying his or her trade in the last 20 years that anyone who can remember flared trousers the first time round need not apply.

Surely, then, Tony McCoy would be the worst kind of winner in terms of the integrity of a poll that seeks to represent hundreds of years of racing history. He is a mere 28 years old, has won 19 fewer titles than Sir Gordon Richards and owes most of his success to a prolific association with the most spectacularly successful trainer of any era, who also happens to have a helicopter.

He lags behind Dettori in terms of personality; behind Piggott in terms of long-standing domination; and he doesn't look as good

'McCoy is the man whose achievements, whether he stops now or in five years' time, are unlikely to be surpassed until such time as the science of bionics renders the human jockey obsolete.'

PETER THOMAS

in a hat as the Queen Mum. But to dismiss McCoy as just another David Beckham – a bright star who has captured the imagination of a generation – is to miss the point entirely.

The greats are the ones who change the nature of the field they are playing on. They take the game to a new level by virtue of their efforts. But whereas, for example, Sir Roger Bannister will be forever remembered as the man who ran the sub-four-minute mile that inspired countless others to surpass his achievements, McCoy is the man whose achievements, whether he stops now or in five or ten years' time, are unlikely to be surpassed until such time as the science of bionics renders the human jockey obsolete.

It is as unnecessary as it is impossible to list all of Anthony Peter McCoy's numerical feats, so often have they been gawped at already. Suffice to say that, since his first jumps winner at Gowran Park in 1994, he has ridden more winners in a season than any other rider (289), completed the fastest 100 and fastest 200, become the winningmost jump jockey of all time (1,822 and counting) and rewritten every book ever written on prize money won and races ridden in a campaign.

But it isn't the numbers *per se* that make the man the marvel that he is. Rather it is the fact that these are numbers which, very few years ago, were regarded as so high as to be not within jump racing's frame of reference.

Stan Mellor took 17 years to pass Fred Winter's record. McCoy whizzed past Richard Dunwoody's imposing tally of 1,699 in less than eight and is now rated odds on to hit the once mythical 300-winner mark by the end of the season.

John Francome rates him an automatic first choice as the best ever, for his unwavering commitment, immense power and insatiable thirst for winners. Punters love AP for the way he translates these qualities into an ability to win races he shouldn't on horses that otherwise wouldn't – be it in a Grade 1 or a seller at Plumpton on a wet and windy Monday.

He wouldn't have achieved his numerical pre-eminence without

Martin Pipe, but he is with Pipe simply because Pipe recognises him as the best.

Statistics can lie, but in this case, they simply bear out what the eye sees and the gut feels: technically, he may be the best by only a short head, but by all other criteria his superiority is almost beyond measure.

As Jon Lees pointed out in Wednesday's *Post*, if this vote were conducted among the general public, Frankie Dettori would win by a landslide.

But it isn't, and he surely won't, because you, the serious racing public, know that AP McCoy is the best jockey and the greatest achiever this game will ever see.

Although AP finished the 2002-03 season with his second best ever total of 256 winners, the latter stages were not entirely happy ones – including a broken collarbone at Cheltenham and another 'failed to finish' in the Grand National.

But those setbacks were only temporary. The loss in April 2003 of his original mentor Billy Rock was something much deeper altogether. Jimmy Walker, our man in Ulster, filed the story.

BILLY ROCK, one of Ulster's best-known trainers and the man who launched Tony McCoy's career, died in hospital in County Antrim on Saturday after a long illness. He was 59.

Not only was Rock one of the great characters of Northern Irish racing, he was also one of the most successful trainers there, with horses like Eddie Wee and Helynsar scoring at the highest level in the 1980s. His Jack High, a winner at Leopardstown, Fairyhouse and Naas, was being prepared for the Punchestown Festival next week.

Apart from his training successes, Rock will always be known as the man who discovered McCoy. Rock was a lifelong friend of McCoy's father Paedar, who said yesterday:

'Billy will be greatly missed. He and I had known each other for as long as I can remember and Tony is shattered by the news.'

McCoy began working for Rock when he was 12, and eventually Rock sent him to Jim Bolger, from where he went to England to begin his meteoric rise to the top.

The champion jockey said: 'Had it not been for Billy Rock, I would never have been in the position I am today. He gave me every opportunity and stood by me at all times. I just can't believe he's gone.'

Jimmy Walker filed another report after the funeral.

AN EMOTIONAL Tony McCoy yesterday spoke of how much he owed his career to trainer Billy Rock, who died on Saturday after a long illness.

The champion jockey was speaking at Rock's funeral in Cullybackey in County Antrim, Northern Ireland.

He said: 'No one will ever know how much I owe to this man. He was my lifetime mentor and nothing was too much trouble for him. I will sorely miss him as a friend.

'As I drove up today to his home and his stables I remembered the time when I rode here on a bicycle and sometimes even walked.

'I was only 12 years old then but I had my mind made up to ride racehorses.

'Billy gave me every encouragement as he was a lifelong friend of my father and knew what racing meant to me.'

Did even Billy Rock realise that racing could mean so much to his protégé that a 250-plus season could be described as a disaster? But that was the unequivocal message in AP's end-of-term report to Jon Lees at Sandown.

FOLLOWING HIS VICTORY on Seebald in the Queen Elizabeth the Queen Mother Celebration Chase, Tony McCoy promised to do better in the latest defence of his jockeys' title that begins today, after describing the 2002-03 season as 'a disaster'.

He takes a ride each at Hexham this afternoon and Newcastle in

AP on Seebald (left) beating Cenkos (Ruby Walsh) in the Queen Elizabeth the Queen Mother Celebration Chase at Sandown Park, 26 April 2003.

the evening as he embarks on his bid to win the crown for the ninth consecutive time.

On Saturday, McCoy equalled Peter Scudamore's record by lifting the title for the eighth time. His haul of 258 wins was his second-highest and his mounts earned prize money of more than £2.5 million.

Along the way he became the winningmost jump jockey of all time and recorded the fastest 200, but he experienced another disappointing Cheltenham Festival in which he concluded the meeting by breaking his collarbone.

As ever Martin Pipe, for whom he won 150 races, will form the backbone of his challenge, in which he will again focus on registering 300 winners. He is 3-1 with William Hill to succeed.

McCoy said: 'I can't wait for the new season to start because last year was a disaster, so next season will hopefully be better. I don't think I had as good a year as the last one or the year before. It can only get better.

'Nothing will change. I will still ride for the same people and I would like to ride 300 winners if I can. I just have to stay injury-free and hope the weather is good through the winter so that I can ride more winners. There isn't a bother with the injury now. Everything is fine.'

McCOY'S SEASON 2002-2003

wins:	258
rides:	840
strike rate:	31%
position in championship:	1st

McCoy helped Pipe to his record 13th trainers' championship and David Johnson to his third owners' title.

'It's a great thrill to win the championship again,' said Pipe, speaking on the Pipeline. 'I had 190 winners but I worked out I beat AP by about £16,000 on prize-money, so that's something I'll have to tease him about!'

Fortunately not everyone shared the multiple champion's dismissal of his achievements. In June 2003 Howard Wright reported:

TONY McCOY'S phenomenal success as a jump jockey has been recognised with an MBE in the Queen's Birthday Honours List, published today.

As he prepared for another day at the office at Newton Abbot yesterday evening, McCoy, typically, sought to involve the sport and those who have helped his career in the award.

'It's a great honour, not just for me but for the whole of jump racing,' he said. 'I couldn't have got it without the help of a lot of people. I just manage to get on the fastest horses. It helps when that happens.'

But Howard also noted a disappointingly muted response beyond the immediate confines of jump racing.

GENERAL MEDIA REACTION to Tony McCoy's deserved MBE showed once again that racing generally figures on news pages only when there is skulduggery or frippery involved.

Taken at random, the *Daily Mail* and *Daily Telegraph* failed to include him in the early-paper round-up of sporting figures in the Honours List, though both covered the award on their sports pages.

Even stranger was the fact that Channel 4's *The Morning Line* took 35 minutes to get round to a mention of McCoy's honour.

If one of our own takes that line, what chance is there for the rest?

Within a week of the royal honour McCoy was facing rather harsher problems than media indifference. He was already on 36 for the season, and seemingly heading for 37, when a horse called Kymberlya crashed down on the final bend at Worcester.

First reports suggested a straightforward broken wrist. Ten days later, at the end of June 2003, Rodney Masters was explaining just how wrong those first reports had been.

TONY McCOY underwent his fourth general anaesthetic in nine days yesterday, as he prepared for surgery to graft skin from a thigh to help seal the troublesome wound of his broken right arm.

Before the latest operation at Swindon's Great Western Hospital, the champion jockey spoke of how side-effects from the anaesthetic and high doses of antibiotics had been more difficult to cope with than the fracture to his lower right arm, which has been plated.

'There were three or four different antibiotics to take and I never knew it was possible to feel so sick in the stomach,' said McCoy.

'The actual break was fine and in a way it hasn't been the issue. It was the effect of the drugs and, at that stage, two general anaesthetics in just a few days.'

McCoy, who was speaking to the *Racing Post*'s Alastair Down for an interview published in the *Sunday Mirror*, said he expected to be out of action for six weeks, 'and I will try not to make the mistake of coming back too early.'

He underwent the initial surgery at Worcester General Hospital for the insertion of a metal plate, stretching almost from wrist to elbow, soon after the fall. He was allowed home, but the following day the arm began to swell, and the jockey was running a temperature and sweating.

'Everything was fine until the arm decided it would try to come out through the plaster on Saturday night.'

McCoy took the opportunity to thank everyone for sending cards and get-well messages. His visitors have included Richard Dunwoody, and Martin Pipe has been a regular caller.

'Pipey has rung every day, concerned at first, but now I'm getting better all he does is wind me up about how far I'll be behind in the jockeys' table when I return.'

The enforced lay-off did at least mean that McCoy and fellow jump jockey Mick Fitzgerald could concentrate on running their first Charity Golf Day – albeit that neither of them were fit to swing a club.

TONY McCOY, Mick Fitzgerald and Adrian Maguire were all out to get one over each other at The Belfry in Birmingham yesterday.

The champion jockey and Fitzgerald, who are handicapped with injuries at present, were holding their inaugural charity golf day.

Teams of four were playing on the PGA National Course for the AP McCoy and Mick Fitzgerald Challenge Trophy, held in aid of the Adrian Maguire Testimonial Fund and the Alder Hey Children's Hospital.

Maguire, whose testimonial year is taking in a series of events, was forced to give up riding after a fall resulted in a serious neck injury.

Now fully recovered but not physically fit enough to resume riding, Maguire is going to Ireland with his family to start a point-to-point training yard.

It was 22 August by the time McCoy was fit to return, and by then he was 18 winners behind perennial rival Richard Johnson in the jockeys' table. After the Gary Moore-trained Flying Spirit had made all the running round Fontwell the lead was only 17. By December McCoy was back in front, and by the middle of January a four-timer at Wincanton had taken him through the 2,000-winner barrier.

But it was not all plain sailing. On New Year's Eve he had received a much disputed five-day suspension for hitting Deano's Beeno an 'excessive' number of times before getting the notoriously reluctant starter to finally consent to race.

The irritation that lingered flared into life when an equally controversial ban was imposed a month later. Andrew King reported from Hereford.

CHAMPION JOCKEY Tony McCoy was left fuming again last night after a ban for his use of the whip when the stewards at Hereford ruled he had caused a weal mark on a horse.

McCoy was banned for one day following a vet's report that his mount The Lyme Volunteer returned marked after finishing runner-up in the extended three-mile handicap chase.

McCoy will miss a meeting at Folkestone, but, despite the size of the punishment, he let out a stream of criticism at the stewards.

He said: 'They have done me under the most stupid rule I've ever heard in my life.

'They seem to make them up as they go along. I'm outraged by what I see as the stupidity of the decision and I'm going to consider an appeal even though I've only got a day. As far as I'm concerned, it's the principle of the matter.

'I'm supposed to have marked the horse, yet I haven't taken my hands off the reins and all I've done is slap the mare down the neck. She has never marked when I've ridden her before.'

Senior stipendiary steward William Nunneley said: 'McCoy has used his whip with excessive frequency and the vet reported to us that the mare returned marked.'

Nunneley was on duty at Cheltenham over the New Year for the controversy that flared when McCoy was banned after the stewards claimed he hit Deano's Beeno 50 times before the start of a race.

Nunneley added: 'He was hitting the horse down the shoulder, albeit in the back-hand, during the final circuit of the race and continued to do so, causing wealing on the horse's shoulder.'

On these sort of occasions, you wondered if some of the frustrations might get McCoy down. Within a couple of days an interview with the At The Races television channel had put the record straight. Rodney Masters reported.

IN A RARE DEPARTURE from his accustomed style of self-deprecation, Tony McCoy let slip yesterday that he reckons that over recent weeks he has ridden 'as well as I have for a long time.'

> 'They have done me under the most stupid rule I've ever heard in my life.'
>
> TONY McCOY

131

Over that period, the champion's winners included an acclaimed performance on the unpredictable Puntal at Ascot, and a hat-trick at Taunton, where he earned the plaudits for a strong ride on Your So Cool.

Less than a month ago he registered his 2,000th winner in Britain.

In an interview with At The Races, McCoy was asked to compare his riding now with three years ago. 'I think over the last fortnight or so I've been riding as well as I have for a long time,' he replied.

McCoy stressed that there will be no let-up in his schedule because he wanted to put his records beyond the reach of future champions, and he said he will not slow down to become a cherry-picker of Saturday rides.

'I enjoy a Monday at the Plumptons and Fontwells with three or four good rides – I genuinely enjoy it,' he said.

'When I don't enjoy it I'll not do it. When I don't want to do it on a Monday then I'll not want to do it on a Saturday.'

With his ongoing partnership with Martin Pipe, McCoy emphasised that 300 winners in a season remained an ambition.

He came within 11 of the triple century in the 2001-02 season, but has been denied the opportunity this time because of the broken arm that put him on the sidelines earlier in the campaign.

'I'll need a lot of things to go right for the 300, and I probably don't get the same constant supply of outside rides I did, although this season has been good in that respect,' he said.

'Certain stables have more established young jockeys coming along and obviously trainers like the commitment and to have someone on hand, which is understandable. You don't ride for them as much as you did.'

Although he did not mention Jonjo O'Neill as an example of the latter, the emergence of home-grown talent Liam Cooper at Jackdaws Castle has seen less demand for McCoy's services from that quarter.

With Chanelle Burke (later Chanelle McCoy) after collecting the award for Jump Jockey of the Year at 'The Lesters' – the Jockeys' Association annual awards evening – in January 2004.

McCoy went to Musselburgh for five rides yesterday and returned home on the same score as he started the day, 155, to stay eight clear of Richard Johnson in the race for the jockeys' title.

The 'I still love Plumpton' line was soon put to the test. Reporters have to get used to falls and to trying to match grim-sounding medical details with optimistic reports from the riders. At Plumpton on 16 February 2004, Neil Morrice had to do his best.

TONY McCOY suffered a major injury scare in the run-up to the Cheltenham Festival after fracturing his left cheekbone in three places in a nasty fall at Plumpton yesterday.

Doctors at the Princess Royal Hospital in Haywards Heath, West Sussex, told him the news last night following his fall from Polar Red at the second fence in the Tyser Insurance Ltd Novices' Chase.

The champion jockey had x-rays on the injury, caused by a kick in the face, and left hospital clutching an ice pack to his cheek, having been put on painkillers.

The fracture will require surgery, which McCoy is keen to have carried out by his own specialist Dr Michael Foy, but the jockey

Overleaf: Face in the mirror.

133

was in optimistic mood and is looking for a quick return to action, possibly in a matter of days rather than weeks.

McCoy, his face bruised under the left eye and with a long graze to his swollen cheek, said: 'It's the first time I have sustained an injury like this but I feel fine and could ride tomorrow if I had to. I shall need an operation but I want to get it done at home and will know more after I've spoken to Dr Turner [the Jockey Club's chief medical officer].

'I hope to be back in a few days and that, if necessary, I can wear a mask for protection. They let people use them for rugby and football and I see no reason why the same can't be true for a jockey.'

When told that McCoy may have sustained a broken cheekbone, Dr Michael Turner said: 'Broken cheekbones tend to be straightforward, unless they have to operate. Usually you get a nice black eye and a swelling. Any broken bone tends to take four to six weeks to heal. The vast majority of cheekbones come good very quickly. I would be cautiously optimistic that he would be back for the Festival.'

However, Jockey Club spokesman John Maxse said it was 'unlikely' McCoy would be allowed to wear any kind of protective mask.

The Cheltenham Festival starts in exactly four weeks and last night it was thought unlikely that McCoy's injury would prevent him from competing at the most prestigious meeting of the season.

Dr Gautam Ray, who attended to McCoy at the hospital, said: 'Tony will require an operation which, under normal circumstances, would mean one night in hospital. He shall be speaking to his local surgeons tomorrow before deciding where to have the operation.'

McCoy was driven home by Mark Bradburne following a miserable day for the jockey. He had earlier suffered a heavy fall from Tanterari in the Whippers Delight Novices' Chase, while his mount Flying Wanda, odds-on for the novices' hurdle, struggled into fourth after making mistakes.

Opposite: 'I've got to wear a plaster on my face to make sure no mud or whatever gets in the wound.' Back in action on Jardin Fleuri at Ludlow, 25 February 2004.

'Pain is what you let it be.'

TONY McCOY

By any standards AP was not a pretty sight, but in very short time Andrew King was relating business as usual.

THE INDOMITABLE Tony McCoy bounced straight back from nine days off with a fractured cheekbone by riding a double at Ludlow yesterday, although he had a scare with a heavy fall in the last.

The first race may have been only a lowly selling hurdle but McCoy showed no ring-rustiness as the Martin Pipe-trained Jardin Fleuri was being pushed and shoved along from some way out.

At the last, his mount was being strongly challenged by Cody, but that rival departed, leaving Jardin Fleuri to hold the renewed challenge of Ben More by a head. The champion said: 'I'm still sore and bruised and I don't look pretty. I've got to wear a plaster on my face to make sure no mud or whatever gets in the wound, but that's all it is, a plaster.

'Basically, it's a case of it all being in the head, and pain is what you let it be. If I thought I was going to make a fool of myself I wouldn't have come back, but I'm here because I want to be.'

Despite his recent lay-off and another three-month enforced rest during the summer with a broken arm, McCoy said he was pleased with the way the remainder of the season had gone.

He added: 'I'm happy with the way I've been riding, regardless of the injuries this term, and the day I go home and watch the video at night and I'm not happy with myself I'll be gone. That will be it, I'll retire.'

McCoy went on to complete a double when Ken'tucky, trained by Nicky Henderson, beat Tribal Dancer in the staying handicap hurdle.

But he was brought back down to earth with a bump with a heavy fall from Kercabellec at the fifth in the concluding novices' hurdle. Returning in the ambulance, he eventually limped into the jockeys' shower room none the worse.

AP got himself ready but the big winners would not come, and the Grand National served up what was becoming a traditional disappointment when co-favourite Jurancon turned over at the fourth.

But the pickings were not that lean. On 12 April 2004 Bruce Jackson reported another milestone from what had been an eventful Plumpton that season.

TONY McCOY reached an 'unlikely' 200 winners for the season at Plumpton yesterday and reaffirmed his desire to become the first jockey to hit 300 in one campaign.

Few of his 200 have come easier than on Tucacas, who justified her 2-5 price in style in the novices' chase.

The eight-time champion jockey, who will be crowned again in 13 days' time, was completing the double century for the fourth time in the last five years and the fifth time in total, but reflected on further lost opportunities.

McCoy rued the time lost this season through his arm and cheekbone injuries and two costly suspensions that ruled him out for a total of three and a half months, without which he would almost certainly have been posting a similar score to the last two seasons.

A year ago to the day he posted 250, with a winner at Ludlow on his way to 258, and the year before was his record-breaking season when he finished with 289 winners.

McCoy, who suffered his cheekbone injury at Plumpton in February, said: 'I have had a long time off this winter with my arm and cheek and big suspensions, including the Deano's Beeno one, so I definitely didn't think I could reach 200.

'It has been a harder season than most for that reason and if you can ride 200 you have to be very pleased.

'I still think 300 is possible and if I hadn't had so much time off I might have been close – having three and a half months off I'd like to think I have missed a few winners in that time!'

Plumpton marked McCoy's achievement with course owner and BHB chairman Peter Savill presenting him with crystal candlesticks.

McCoy, paying tribute to both Martin Pipe and his agent Dave Roberts, added that his commitment to riding winners day in and day out remained undiminished and promptly proved it, as he remounted last-fence faller Trade Off to finish second two races later.

McCoy has also reached 200 in 1997-98, 1999-2000, 2001-02 and last season. No other jump jockey has achieved consecutive double centuries, but McCoy still has some way to go to equal Sir Gordon Richards' record of 12 double centuries.

These are the statistics of the superstar, but no jockey is a hero to the disgruntled punter who has backed him on a loser – as McCoy was reminded at Ayr a few days later, with Tom O'Ryan on hand to witness.

TONY McCOY was keen to defend his corner after suffering verbal abuse from a punter after the two-mile handicap chase.

McCoy, who had just finished third on a tired Golden Alpha, was angered by the remarks from the racegoer, who was standing a few yards outside the winner's enclosure.

Leaving his horse unsaddled, he went over to the rails to confront the man, who was quickly surrounded by two policemen.

McCoy said: 'This punter started swearing and shouting abuse at me and I don't see why I should take it, so I decided to stand my corner. He can't know much about the game as anyone who backs Golden Alpha on soft ground must be mad.'

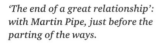

'The end of a great relationship': with Martin Pipe, just before the parting of the ways.

Disgruntled punters will never change, but even the most solid of trainer-jockey partnerships can alter with the years. There had been rumours for a while of a parting of the Pipe and McCoy ways – but it was still a shock when Neil Morrice reported it for us at the end of April.

McCOY'S SEASON 2003-2004	
wins:	209
rides:	800
strike rate:	26%
position in championship:	1st

THE NEED FOR a new challenge and the lure of a huge financial incentive finally persuaded Tony McCoy to end his record-breaking link to champion trainer Martin Pipe in favour of Jonjo O'Neill, it emerged yesterday.

O'Neill and JP McManus, his landlord and principal owner, were believed last night to have offered McCoy what one close source put at a staggering £1 million a year.

Others placed the figure at a more conservative £300,000, but even at that Pipe found he could not compete for McCoy's professional affections.

A fuller picture of McCoy's shock move came from the principals themselves, but only after unprecedented secrecy and denials during Wednesday before the truth could be hidden no longer.

The firm messages were that Pipe and McCoy are parting on good terms, and that O'Neill is excited at the prospect of adding champion trainer to his status as champion jockey.

McCoy, riding at Hereford, said he was ready to launch himself into 'an exciting new challenge' while admitting the decision was the most difficult he had ever had to make.

He said his agreement to ride for O'Neill did not involve a contract that would commit him to the Jackdaws Castle operation of legendary owner and gambler McManus for any specific time.

Though the lure of O'Neill's top-flight jumpers is obvious, there can be little doubt the nine-time champion was 'helped' by a retainer expected to be the biggest ever in jump racing.

McCoy said: 'I saw Jonjo on Tuesday and only spoke to him then about the new job before I told Martin the following day. The job is to ride as first jockey for Jonjo O'Neill and there was no question of a contract, as I just don't do them.

'The move is not about money but about a different challenge and a different way of life, and if we can build Jackdaws Castle into a super force it will be fantastic.

'When I told Martin, he was gutted, and so was I – it's the end of a great relationship. But the job I'm taking is something that excites me, although I appreciate how much harder it will be to retain my title and to even think about riding 300 winners in a season is inconceivable without the assistance of Martin.'

McCoy expects to ride for Pipe on occasions in the future. 'The decision was the toughest thing I've ever had to do in my life,' he said. 'If you're allowed to ride for Martin Pipe as stable jockey, the one thing you know is that he always has a plan that is so far ahead you could never even think of keeping up with him.

'I really don't know who Martin will choose as his new jockey, but every jockey in the country owes it to himself to be ringing up for the job.'

Although McCoy is about to reach his 30th birthday, he added: 'I feel younger and fitter and fresher than ever, and if I stay in one piece whoever takes away my title will have to ride a massive number of winners to do it.'

Paying tribute to Pipe, he added: 'I called in again on Martin last night and we remain the best of friends. I'm so very lucky in that he's been such a gent in every sense.'

O'Neill was ecstatic at having landed McCoy. 'We're delighted to have him,' he said. 'He'll have first call on our horses and will have the pick of the rides. We're all excited Tony will be on the team. We want him to stay champion and, hopefully, we'll help him do that.

'He starts for us at Worcester tomorrow. We weren't going to start him off at a big track like Punchestown – it might give him a big head!'

O'Neill added: 'Of course I'd love to be champion trainer – we just need more winners.'

And Jon Lees reflected on 'the most prolific partnership in jump racing history'.

CLASSIC SERVICE FOR PUNTERS

1,000 Guineas –
The Gang of Four
deliver their verdicts,
pages 14-15

Plus –
a free £20 bet
for EVERY reader,
page 20

The Oaks –
Pricewise with a
14-1 selection,
pages 20-21

RACING POST

Friday, April 30, 2004
Issue No. 5,787

WWW.RACINGPOST.CO.UK

£1.20

A new dawn

McCoy switches to O'Neill in big-money McManus deal – see pages 2-5

● Jonjo strikes at Punchestown with Rhinestone Cowboy, pages 16-17

● Champion Hurdle hero Hardy Eustace in Rooster Booster rematch, page 10

AP LEAVES MP TO JOIN JP. The initial difference may be minor but the implications major for the career of the outstanding jockey Tony McCoy.

Calling an end to what Martin Pipe himself yesterday described as 'one of the best partnerships ever in racing history' will not have been easy, but what other decision could he make when promised such riches?

During eight years in partnership, Pipe helped McCoy rewrite the record books. They were an ideal match and, though their parting was amicable and no tears were shed, there is bound to be some regret.

Most of us would not hesitate in accepting a job that offered a substantial increase in income, but McCoy's disclosure that his decision to leave marked 'one of the saddest days of my career' reveals the depth of the relationship.

The winners will keep flowing for McCoy – he may still continue to reign as champion jockey – but as genial as his boss Jonjo O'Neill

> 'Pipe trained the horses, McCoy rode them, and each implicitly trusted the other to carry out their task.'
>
> JON LEES

is, it is unlikely AP will develop as strong a bond as he has with the master of Pond House.

The pair will have experienced their highs and lows – all relationships do – but there have been few cross words between the two during their long and highly successful association.

Even when it was over, they spoke warmly of one another. McCoy described Pipe as 'a genius', Pipe said the jockey had been 'brilliant'.

McCoy was 21 when he succeeded David Bridgwater as Pipe's stable jockey. In his first season in Britain, attached to Toby Balding, he had won the conditional jockeys' title with a then record 74 wins and had been champion jockey the following season.

Pipe, already a multiple champion trainer, had enjoyed prolific success with former stable jockeys Peter Scudamore and then Richard Dunwoody, but in union with McCoy their feats reached another level.

In their first campaign together, McCoy helped Pipe break David Nicholson's two-year spell as champion trainer and established a trend that they have sustained ever since.

Like-minded people, they are both driven men, both possess a burning desire to be first every time and have utter respect for each other's abilities. They are also friends.

Pipe trained the horses, McCoy rode them, and each implicitly trusted the other to carry out their task. Pipe never tied his jockey down with orders and McCoy knew the horses were produced fit to run to their best.

In harness they established the most prolific partnership in jump racing history. At the end of last season McCoy won his ninth jockeys' title in a row, while Pipe finished top of the trainers' table for the fourteenth time in the last 16 years.

Despite suffering a broken arm last June and a fractured cheekbone in February, McCoy still beat off the challenge of Richard Johnson to take the 2003-04 championship with 209 winners, of which Pipe supplied 116.

In the last season, McCoy registered his 2,000th winner in

January on the Pipe-trained Magical Bailiwick, less than ten years after he arrived in Britain from Ireland. In 2002 he beat Sir Gordon Richards' all-time record total of 269 winners in a season and the following campaign established himself as the all-time winningmost jumps jockey, beating Richard Dunwoody's 1,699.

In 1997, McCoy rode Make A Stand to victory in the Champion Hurdle, which still remains the big-race highlight of the Pipe-McCoy association.

Yet there have been numerous other triumphs, especially at the Cheltenham Festival, where in 1998 McCoy equalled the record of five wins by a jockey, helped by victories on the Pipe-trained Champleve, Blowing Wind, Cyfor Malta and Unsinkable Boxer.

They will both have taken immense satisfaction from the way Pipe, written off in the 2003-04 championship race when adrift of rival Paul Nicholls approaching this year's Festival, clawed back the deficit to eventually take the title convincingly.

The campaign roll of honour for the season just ended was a Pipe 'family' affair. Martin Pipe champion trainer, Tony McCoy champion jockey, David Johnson champion owner and Jamie Moore champion conditional.

Maybe a fitting time to move on to something else.

A new challenge, in McCoy's words. An end of an era in ours.

Would O'Neill provide enough of the 'winner fuel' which the McCoy machine needs to function? Would the now 30-year-old multiple champion begin to be slightly more selective with his rides and maybe a touch more careful with himself? Would this latest move herald a short and final chapter?

These were legitimate questions. For us it is a joy to be able to bring you so full and golden a set of answers. As the instruction books say, 'Please read on.'

McMANUS

T*he arrangement with JP McManus and Jonjo O'Neill started off with enough winners to keep AP clear of his rivals, but it was not to be an untroubled season in several respects.*

As usual we were reporting injuries – but writer and jockey almost had smiles on their faces with this report from Rodney Masters at the end of August.

TONY McCOY injured his left ankle in a charity football match yesterday at the Greatwood open day in Wiltshire but, ever defiant, is confident of being fit to ride at Huntingdon today.

A lump the size of a golf ball appeared rapidly on the outside of the champion's ankle, and it was immediately packed in ice.

'It's sore enough but I've ridden with worse and I'll be OK to take my rides tomorrow,' he said.

'I broke a bone in the same ankle playing football a couple of years ago, and the next day I rode a couple of winners.'

He was later driven home by a friend with the injured ankle covered by a blue bag of ice.

The damage was done shortly before half-time in a jockeys versus trainers match, which is one of the highlights of the annual open day at the Racehorse Rehabilitation Centre near Marlborough.

McCoy turned suddenly in the middle of the pitch and soon realised that he had a problem. He limped off and took no further part in the match. The trainers won on penalties.

The injury meant McCoy had no time to reacquaint himself with his old sparring partner Deano's Beeno, the enigmatic hurdler who was retired to the Greatwood Centre in the summer after an honourable career spanning 11 seasons, during which he won more than £250,000.

If McCoy could get himself injured off the track, he could also find new – and extremely painful – ways of getting himself injured on it. Just think of running the reins through your fingers when you read this one, reported in the Racing Post *on 16 November 2004 …*

Previous spread: In the JP McManus colours.

TONY McCOY was determined to be back in action for the Hennessy Gold Cup meeting a week on Saturday after dislocating his thumb in an accident at Folkestone yesterday – an injury that had initially threatened to rule him out until Christmas.

Examination of a suspected broken right thumb, damaged when he fell off and was dragged on the way to the start of a juvenile hurdle, proved it to be a less serious injury to the digit's tip.

Although it rules McCoy out of a planned reunion with Edredon Bleu in Saturday's Totesport Peterborough Chase at Huntingdon, he was intent on making himself available for the following weekend at Newbury, where he is due to cement a new partnership with star staying hurdler Baracouda.

McCoy's thumb was caught in the reins after he was unshipped from the Gary Moore-trained Flying Patriarch. His personal assistant Gee Armytage later said: 'There is no fracture. He dislocated the tip of his thumb, which has been put back tonight by hand specialist Ian Lowdon.

'Tony did say he was thinking of taking part in the race because the injury wasn't that bad. Ian Lowdon said he was very hopeful that Tony could be back within a fortnight.

'AP, being AP, would want to be back for the Hennessy. AP is very tough and is in his usual upbeat mood and is determined not to be off for very long.'

At first it was feared the injury was serious enough to put McCoy on the sidelines up to Christmas and possibly beyond, putting his championship challenge on hold for a considerable time.

Speaking straight after the accident, McCoy said: 'I was tying the reins when another horse came galloping past and my horse took off. I was thinking about riding in the race – the thumb isn't sore – but when I took my glove off at the start I thought I'd better not.'

Dr Peter Magauran, the racecourse doctor, said: 'He had a laceration. We treated him with a local anaesthetic and gave him painkillers. The thumb now needs to be set and immobilised. In my opinion he'll be out of action for six to eight weeks.'

> 'AP is very tough and is in his usual upbeat mood and is determined not to be off for very long.'
>
> GEE ARMYTAGE

149

But the real pains in this first post-Martin Pipe season were more mental than physical. For while the new Jonjo O'Neill link-up produced plenty of winners during the 'little fish' days of summer, when the big days of autumn came it was soon clear that they were way short of the Pipe ammunition in the big races. And what prospects they had were afflicted by a virus which culminated in Jonjo almost closing down his Jackdaws Castle yard.

In the racing parish it felt like crisis time, and in late November Alastair Down went along to take the temperature.

IT IS testament to Tony McCoy's qualities as a man that it is exceptionally rare to hear a bad word about him. He is revered by his fellow jockeys for his professional talents – but their affection for him is a genuine expression of how they value McCoy as a friend and a man.

However, his legion of admirers throughout racing will have been surprised – and concerned – by the remarks he made in the *Sunday Times* when he said: 'As far as I'm concerned Jackdaws Castle has to move up and, if it doesn't do that, I don't want to be there. Simple as that. But I know Jonjo wants it too.'

The reasons why Tony McCoy is a great jockey are varied, but one quality has contributed more to his success than anything – his ferocious, driven, obsessive, almost psychotic desire to win races. Not just big races, but every race, every day on every sort of course and every type of horse.

It is not that he doesn't like being beaten; he actively hates it. He regards defeat as a cross between a personal insult and a kick in the stomach. He is allergic to being anything else than a winner. AP is chronically addicted to victory.

A lesser man would be ruined by having such an all-consuming monkey on the back. Yet he is not. Time spent in his company is never wasted. He is bright, good fun, endlessly generous and has a hard man's kindness. But occasionally the pressure he puts on himself builds up to such an extent that, like tectonic plates grinding against each other, the forces become so great that an earthquake becomes inevitable.

We have seen it before. Back in 1998 he returned after winning the Mackeson on Cyfor Malta and, at what should have been a moment of happy triumph, scowled his way into the winner's enclosure and hurled his whip into the crowd.

That was at the height of the problems he was having with the Jockey Club over his use of the whip. He felt he was being persecuted and looked an unhappy, hunted and haunted man in need of help. And he got help, from his friends and also the authorities who, realising that he was jumping's totemic figure, went out of their way to make him understand that they were actually on his side. To his great credit McCoy changed his style and that dark period was put behind him.

Then there was the nightmare Festival of 2002 when he went winnerless until Royal Auclair bailed him out in the Cathcart. He never smiled all week and I remember being embarrassed for him that not once did he take part in the time-honoured ritual of congratulating his fellow jockeys who had won at the meeting that means more to them than anything else.

The last few weeks will have been torture for McCoy. His view will be that the move from Martin Pipe has cost him field days at

Cheltenham and Newbury and deprived him of a Paddy Power and a Hennessy. Victory on an ageing hero like Baracouda will have been scant consolation.

But he has made his bed at Jackdaws and must lie in it. JP McManus has assembled probably the greatest arsenal of potential jump stars in the sport's history. Like fine wine, some of them may take time. To ride them, JP has employed the services of the greatest rider of his time.

It is not a Pipe-type set-up and McCoy knew it when he went there. I hate to see a man for whom I have the greatest admiration going through the mill, but nobody is dying here and the results will come – as sure as the sun will rise tomorrow.

It has been a privilege to have been a commentator in the age of McCoy. I was a late convert to his qualities but I am resolute in my support of him. His comments will not have improved morale at Jackdaws, but JP is too wise to let them affect his commitment to the empire he is building there.

AP gets Baracouda up to head Crystal D'Ainay (Robert Thornton) in the Ballymore Properties Long Distance Hurdle at Newbury, 27 November 2004.

Tony McCoy has capacities and virtues the rest of us would give an arm for. He needs to tough it out and nobody I know is better equipped to do so.

Even four months later people were still questioning the wisdom of his pre-season move, but not McCoy himself. Things might be tough, but the sense of fevered crisis that was around in November had gone away. It was now nine full years on from that first interview with Rodney Masters, and in March 2005 Peter Thomas met a much more complete man.

IF YOU thought Benjamin Disraeli had a low opinion of statistics, then don't get Tony McCoy on the subject at the moment. Lies and damned lies don't get a look-in when AP vents his spleen.

'Statistics are shit,' he'll tell you. 'At least mine are at the moment.' You get the feeling he's joking, but you don't really want to ask.

By rights, the champion jockey should be like a bear with a sore head. He's spent the past few months waiting on a bunch of sidelined superstars. And now – indignity of indignities – he's heading into the Festival as a 7-1 shot to be leading jockey. Not quite an *annus horribilis*, but a bit of a bugger, nonetheless, you might think.

The stats, though, paint a rather different picture, and McCoy is surprisingly philosophical when asked to put his year into perspective. He may be a couple of lengths off his usual pace, but this reputedly gloomy individual is a long way from sticking his head in the oven.

'Things aren't going as bad as everyone likes to think. I've had around 170 winners, and although I knew at the start of the season that it's always going to be more difficult to be champion jockey when you're not riding for Martin Pipe, at the same time I thought that if I could get to 200 winners, I'd have a good chance.

'There's a bit of a way to go, but there's a bit of time left, too, so hopefully I can be champion again. And if anybody rides more than that, then fair play to them.

'People forget that at the beginning of the summer, Jonjo got me a lot of winners, and it's unfortunate for him that the horses got sick after that. I think I rode about 70 winners for him early on, which is a big help, and without that, I wouldn't be in contention.

'If I'm lucky enough to be champion, then a lot of it will be down to him, no matter how things have gone lately.'

It looks as though luck won't enter into it. McCoy is 45 winners clear of Timmy Murphy – the man who stepped into the breach at Pipe's – and firmly on course for a ninth successive jockeys' title.

Last year it was a broken arm that restricted him to 209 winners; this year, a poorly timed career move has held him back; but although there has been no talk for some time of the magical 300 mark, there is no suggestion that the fire in the champ's grate is dying.

While some observers judged his move to Jackdaws Castle as being motivated solely by JP McManus's bank account, McCoy is adamant he has no intention of letting it dull his competitive edge.

In fact, he sees in Jonjo O'Neill, his new guv'nor, much of the same steel and ambition that took Pipe to the top.

He says: 'It wasn't a question of me having lost my edge. If I thought that, it wouldn't matter how much anybody was paying me, I couldn't go out and ride a horse if I didn't think I could give it my best, ride it better than the person beside me.

'I want to help take the operation there to the next level, and if I don't do that then I'll consider that I've failed, which isn't something I like or that I've done too often in the past.

'Some people see me as having gone from working for a racing nut to working for a jolly Irishman, but Jonjo isn't as jolly an Irishman as a lot of people think. He'd have a different way with people to Martin, but there's no doubt he wants to succeed.

'He's not just there for the happy life. If he'd just wanted that, he'd have stayed in Penrith.

'Martin sets the standard, but Jonjo has the same kind of drive and I've been as disappointed for him as for myself because I've been lucky enough to carry on and work day in and day out.

'Obviously, on good Saturdays throughout the winter it's difficult to get on good horses in good races, when all the stable jockeys are riding, so you're trying to nip around for what other people don't want and make the best of it.

'But at least I could go out and get on with my job – he had to stay in the yard and look at sick horses.'

For all the compassion and humanity, however, there's no doubt it rests heavy on McCoy to be scratching around for scraps when, by rights, he should be enjoying the richest pickings. He chats at length about coping with the trials at Jackdaws, about the calming influence of McManus, about the good times ahead, but he never looks like a man at peace with his words.

He perches on the edge of his seat, hands clasped together; he lolls backwards, hands behind his head, in a caricature of relaxation; and he starts to talk about the fear that nips at his heels.

He's trying, he says, if not to get the monkeys off his back, at least to control their worst excesses; but while the rest of the world may place great value on positive spin and good PR, McCoy remains a man for whom an easy smile and a chipper soundbite are low on the list of priorities.

He says: 'I don't think I'm as obsessed as people think I am, but if you're lucky enough to get in a position where you win a lot, then the more you win, the more you want it, and it can mean you end up acting like a spoilt child when you don't win.

'You have to learn to realise that you can't win all the time.

'I don't know what it is. Every day since I started riding, and more so since I started riding more and more winners, I think you become frightened, as much as anything else, of it all ending.

'Some people go to sports psychologists to get that kind of attitude, and perhaps I need one to help me get rid of it, but I don't think any of them could ever help me. Maybe I need help on the bad days, but I'm just not very good at accepting it.

'Sometimes I wish I could come back home and accept the fact that these things happen. But I don't think, however much I sat down with someone, I could get it out of my head.

'I don't think I'm as obsessed as people think I am.'

TONY McCOY

155

'I think from time to time that I may look back in 15 years and wish I'd enjoyed it more than I did, but I do enjoy it.

'I enjoy it every time I win. I don't know whether it's relief or enjoyment, but I feel I'm very lucky. I'm well aware that I've been very lucky; much as I complain, or I look like I complain, I feel lucky.

'I'm just not great when I go racing, and of late I've been trying to smile a bit more and look happier. I've been told it's the thing to do, if you look a bit happier and cope a bit better, but I still don't think I'm as bad as people say.

'If I have five losers on a Saturday, I might come home and say that's a Saturday and no winners, you know, but I can still go out at night with the lads and have a craic with them. If I was ever going to be miserable, I'd never go out.'

For most of us, 30 would be a bit early to be thinking about retirement – strictly on economic grounds.

At that age, McCoy is well set financially, with a lovely house, a healthy property portfolio and a rosy outlook. But a life of leisure, of watching the Arsenal and strolling round the golf course, is not a prospect he's prepared to entertain, even when pushed.

For a sportsman with a wilfully restricted field of vision, it can come as a shock to take off the blinkers and stare into the void. Having been cocooned by restless ambition ever since he left home in Antrim at fifteen to be ground into shape by Jim Bolger, McCoy will one day have the big, wide world to face up to, but he'd rather meet it later than sooner.

He says: 'At the moment, all I'm frightened of is not riding as many winners as I did the previous year, but it's also what makes me happy. I don't know what I'm going to do when I finish because I don't ever like to consider it.

'You're a long time retired and I've no doubt that whatever I do after this, I'll never enjoy it as much and I'll never have what I have now, so I'd rather not really think about it.'

In the meantime, everything is geared towards prolonging this most prolific of careers. Whereas fellow 'racing freak' Richard Dunwoody liked to keep an iron grip of all aspects of his day-to-day routine, McCoy is happy to relinquish control of everything except what happens in the saddle.

With Dave Roberts booking his rides, Gee Armytage running his life, and a driver who also acts as his golf coach, AP need only point the horses in the right direction – which is fine by him.

'I always thought I didn't want to have to worry about the other things in my life. I always say that I was born to ride horses, not to do the dishes [mildly embarrassed laughter].

'If I'd wanted to be an accountant, then I'd have been an accountant – although I probably wouldn't have been intelligent enough – but I wanted to be a jockey.

'I want to go racing and ride winners and ask other people to do the other things for me, and make it as easy as possible for me, so I can have a chance of enjoying my job longer and lasting longer.'

If the years had produced a slightly more philosophical stance, Cheltenham (not a single winner!) and Aintree came to test it. For the Grand National provided the cruellest cut yet. With the favourite Clan Royal clear and jumping well, this eleventh National was finally going to be the successful one – then, running down to Becher's second time, the ultimate nightmare struck . A loose horse ran right across at the last moment and wiped out Clan Royal so completely that the horse had to refuse and McCoy ended on the Liverpool turf.

But we all knew by now that it takes much, much more than an errant loose horse, albeit on the largest stage of all, to keep McCoy from coming through triumphant.

The 2004-05 season officially ended at Sandown in April, and for a man at one time supposedly so beleaguered, it closed with a crescendo, as Bruce Jackson reported.

AS EVER, Tony McCoy's timing was impeccable. On the last day of the season, and with what turned out to be his last winner of the season, the now ten-time champion jockey completed his fifth double-century when booting home Yes Sir to the cheers of the packed Sandown stands in the opening handicap hurdle.

> 'If I'd wanted to be an accountant, then I'd have been an accountant – although I probably wouldn't have been intelligent enough – but I wanted to be a jockey.'
>
> TONY McCOY

By forcing Yes Sir home by a length and a quarter, McCoy not only reached the notable milestone, but also ensured that former boss Martin Pipe was denied victory, after the trainer's seven-horse attack – reduced from ten following three morning withdrawals – was led by runner-up Penny Pictures.

'I thought the one I was riding was a little better than most of Martin's,' said McCoy, explaining why he had deserted the man who, until he switched to Jonjo O'Neill and JP McManus this season, was his boss.

Describing the chase to get 200 winners as 'hard work' in a campaign in which O'Neill's string was laid low for weeks, McCoy added: "I was lucky that Jonjo and JP got me a good start, and it was unfortunate for them that the horses got sick.

'Dave Roberts [McCoy's agent] did a brilliant job and I'm lucky that I rode a lot of winners for everyone else. In the last two weeks I've been riding for Paul Nicholls and Martin Pipe.'

AP's fifth double-century is landed as Yes Sir (right) wins the Betfred 'The Bonus King' Handicap Hurdle at Sandown Park, 23 April 2005.

'I always knew it would be harder to be champion jockey not riding for Martin, but I set myself the target of riding 200 winners and I knew that if I could do that I had a good chance of being champion jockey.'

The formerly hidden – and to some slightly surprising – secret that behind the goggled ruthlessness of the jockey's face lurked an interesting and kindly human being was beginning to leak out a little, as these three items underline.

McCOY'S SEASON 2004-2005	
wins:	200
rides:	821
strike rate:	24%
position in championship:	1st

A CHARITY that helps to make the wishes of terminally ill children come true is set to be the main benefactor from the £2,000 Tony McCoy won as part of a sponsorship deal between the *Racing Post*, Racing UK and the Jockeys' Association to support the jump jockeys' championship. McCoy picked up £10 for each of the 200 winners he rode in the 2004-05 season, and his assistant Gee Armytage said that the Starlight Children's Foundation is in line for a windfall as part of a three-way split.

'We're going to split up where it goes,' Armytage said. 'Charlie Egerton is going to run next year's London Marathon in aid of the Starlight Children's Foundation, so we have told him that we'll donate some money to them now and if he doesn't run in the race he'll have to give them the same amount himself.

'Tony is also giving some money to his local church in Kingston Lisle, and a bit will go to Belinda Meade, the daughter of ex-jockey Gordon Cramp, whose husband died leaving her with six young children.'

THANK YOU to everyone who has helped me through a season in which I was lucky enough to ride another 200 winners and retain the champion jockeys' title.

It is great that our championship is now sponsored again, and the help of the *Racing Post* and Racing UK is much appreciated.

I could not have achieved this on my own, and I am very grateful to all who have supported me throughout the season.

> 'Tony is a very
> fine human being,
> unspoilt by success.
> He truly graces the
> sport of jump racing.'
>
> SEAMUS KELLY

A big thank you to Jonjo O'Neill, JP McManus and all the other owners and, indeed, the whole team at Jackdaws Castle. They have all been wonderful through what has been a tough time for them and I hope together we can have a successful new season.

Special thanks go to my agent, Dave Roberts, who works so hard on my behalf and has the toughest job of all putting up with me, and to all my valets and weighing-room colleagues who also have to put up with me day in, day out.

Last, a mention for Tom Doyle, who, since the beginning of the new season, has already ridden three winners and assures me he is the main danger to my crown!

He was asleep in the ambulance room, conserving his energy, before riding at Towcester, and his caring fellow jockeys pinned up a notice saying: 'Quiet please, champ sleeping'! Following his most recent triumph, I received a text message from him simply saying: 'Be afraid, be very afraid!' So good luck to Tom.

But back to the reason of my writing: thank you again everybody for your support. It is greatly appreciated.

TONY McCOY
Wantage, Oxon

BEFORE the meeting at Worcester on August 5, I wrote to Tony McCoy asking if it would be possible to meet him in the weighing room before racing.

A few days later his personal assistant Gee Armytage rang me to say Tony would be delighted to meet me and my wife Christina. So, before the first race, with great excitement in our hearts, we went up to meet the greatest ever jumps rider and found him a totally sincere, warm person who was concerned only with our enjoyment of the afternoon.

He gave kindly and freely of his time, and even posed for photos with us.

Tony is a very fine human being, unspoilt by success. He truly

graces the sport of jump racing and my wife and I thank him for
giving us a day we will remember and cherish evermore.

Thank you Tony and God go with you.

SEAMUS KELLY
Worcester

*But if a kinder face was emerging from behind the public mask it
certainly wasn't a softer or – as this dispatch from Geoff Lester in
December 2005 shows – a prettier one.*

TONY McCOY does not believe in requesting a day off, but he
will be forced to find an hour or two tomorrow morning before
Warwick to visit his dentist after having his teeth smashed in a fall
from Risk Accessor in the Robin Cook Memorial Gold Cup.

However, it takes more than the odd tumble to convince McCoy
to take an early bath, and the eight-time champion rode through
the pain barrier to win the Brit Insurance Novices' Hurdle for Jonjo
O'Neill on Black Jack Ketchum.

Named after an American outlaw from yesteryear, Black Jack
Ketchum stretched his unbeaten sequence to five in the Grade 2
contest – three over hurdles and two in bumpers – when outpacing
Gungadu from the last for another easy win.

Reflecting on his injury, McCoy said: 'It's not too bad. I got a
nasty bang at the top of my mouth and they think I might have a
small fracture of the gum, but you forget the pain when you ride
winners.

'My face could have been broken to bits and I would have come
out to ride this lad. I love this little horse. He was always doing just
enough and he has a great attitude about life.'

*This remains the only time that I have heard the public
announcement, 'Is there a dentist on the track?' And the saga of the
next few days will stay exceptional even by McCoy standards.*

On the Sunday following the Cheltenham teeth saga he flew to

Ireland for four rides and another fall. On Monday he had two unsuccessful rides at Plumpton followed by having the root canals fixed in four hours in the dentist's chair. More rides at Warwick on Tuesday before a teetotal trip to a London gala to support Richard Dunwoody ended horrifically in the early hours back home, when he was seized by a shivering fit and was ambulanced to hospital with fears of meningitis and a virus around the heart.

Cue a few recuperative weeks in the sun? When Windsor was abandoned on the Saturday, our hero flogged up to Haydock to ride a beast with the supremely appropriate name of Don't Push It to take the last.

In the circumstances, Don't Push It's Grand National-winning effort for McCoy in 2010 was no more than a favour repaid.

Yet as we progress through this book you should be getting used to the fact that this unusual life still clings to its moments of pleasure, despite all the years of self denial. One of life's finest of all pleasures was beckoning: witness this cryptic report from The Dikler – the closest the Racing Post *has to a gossip column – in January 2006.*

IT WILL be racing's wedding of the year, but where's the venue?

We know Tony McCoy will wed Chanelle Burke in September, but there's plenty of guessing going on whether it'll be held in Ireland, Britain or perhaps Barbados at the Sandy Lane Hotel, part-owned by his paymaster, JP McManus.

The answer is none of the above, as The Dikler is reliably informed the ceremony will be in Majorca.

Fortunately, nowhere near the fish-and-chip shops and Brit bars, but in the tiny village of Deia, which is hidden away in the Tramuntana mountains and is said to have a stunning view of the Mediterranean.

The village holds special memories for the couple, who have been together for nine years.

If you are one of the 50 guests to receive an invitation – and The Dikler isn't holding his breath – it may be handy to know that Deia is one hour's drive from Palma airport.

Opposite: AP's first Cheltenham Festival winner in the JP McManus colours: returning on Reveillez – with the owner on the right – after the Jewson Novices' Handicap Chase, 16 March 2006.

McCOY'S SEASON 2005-2006	
wins:	178
rides:	828
strike rate:	21%
position in championship:	1st

There was plenty of business to be completed before that most important knot could be tied in September. An eleventh championship with the 'comparatively' low score of 178 winners was duly logged in April 2006. The Grand National had given moments of hope before Clan Royal finally finished third, and so the seasonal highlight had to be Brave Inca's unforgettable Champion Hurdle – which saw Alastair Down in unbeatable form.

SUPER-TOUGH and lazier than a siesta-intent Mexican after a tequila lunch, Brave Inca dug deep into the seams only he can mine when battling his way to Champion Hurdle victory.

Born to run up this hill, he has an equally stubborn and remorseless ally in AP McCoy, who won't take no for an answer from Brave Inca and just knows that the more you ask him the more he will come up with.

This was a magnificent Champion Hurdle. The winner is a template for tenacity, Macs Joy was smuggled as close as humanly possible under a wonderfully wily ride from Barry Geraghty while, back in third, Hardy Eustace overcame the sea of troubles that had been his preparation with a sterling run that earned him the most tremendous reception when Conor O'Dwyer brought him back to the place reserved for the third.

But that sound was as nothing compared with the serial walls of sound that crashed out to greet the exultant McCoy, standing high in the stirrups and orchestrating the noise of the packed steppings as he returned on a winner who, indeed, wasn't foaled so much as quarried.

What sets this horse apart from others is that he thrives on the unusual diet of biting off more than he can reasonably be expected to chew. After the triumphs of his novice season, last year was pure hard labour with no remission. Four times in a row he was second before a hammer and tongs third, beaten two necks in the Champion, followed by a crashing fall at Aintree.

And proper races they were – not egg-and-spoons at the village fete-worse-than-death or the sack race at the school sports. Every time he ran was against top-class opposition in the most fearsomely contested events.

Many horses would have been soured by so many repeated bashings of head against brick walls. But Colm Murphy thinks that long, hard season with his line in the most turbulent of waters was actually the making of Brave Inca.

If you were to sit down and design a horse for McCoy, this is the one you would come up with. His almost implausible toughness strikes a chord with the champion, who looked far from happy early on in yesterday's race. He was having to keep Brave Inca at it, and said: 'I got in a bit deep at the second last but he pricked his ears going to it and I thought "You've got loads left!"'

Implicit in that remark was McCoy's reaction, which would have been 'And I'm just the man to get it out of you, old bollocks!'

'Born to run up this hill': Brave Inca wins the Smurfit Kappa Champion Hurdle, 14 March 2006.

The heroes' return.

Once Brave Inca had hit the front, despite the battling Hardy Eustace still being bang on the premises and Macs Joy stalking and going well, there was only going to be one result, as this horse is not for passing. He possesses untold amounts of courage – if he were a military man he'd be a Gurkha – and while his natural laziness to eke out his brilliance like a miser means he never has an easy race, it ensures that when a rival gets to him he always finds more. He never pulls one rabbit out of the hat, they come out one after another in a demoralising stream until the opposition can take no more.

When Murphy said: 'Whoever got by him today would have known they had a race', he was speaking nothing but the truth, but the thing about Brave Inca this season is that they simply aren't passing him any more.

The new title holder doesn't do wide-margin victories, and that quirk may mean his superiority continues to be underrated. But, with two mega wins in Ireland this winter and yesterday's crowning achievement, he is very much the best around, despite the apparent narrowness of superiority on the form book.

He looked awesomely well in the paddock and has a heart as big as a house. AP said simply: 'I love him.' Judging from the way the Cheltenham crowd took Brave Inca to their hearts yesterday, he is not alone.

It may have been very much more by accident than design, but that summer AP did contrive to take an almost two-month wedding break. The accident was a badly broken wrist at Galway at the beginning of August, and it was not until Hereford at the end of September that racegoers saw him in action once again.

You will hardly need to guess at the results.

TONY McCOY made an immediate impact on his return to action after eight weeks off when taking the opening novice hurdle on Absolutelythebest to bring up his 50th win of the season, then doubling up on Bouncy Castle in the bumper.

McCoy's season had been abruptly interrupted by the broken wrist he suffered in a fall from Sporting Limerick at the Galway festival, and ever since he has been like a caged tiger waiting to be allowed back to the wild.

'As soon as I hit the ground at Galway my first thought was how long was I going to be out,' he said. 'It's been heartbreaking missing those weeks, but great to come back with a winner. John O'Shea said Absolutelythebest was in tip-top form, and he was right.'

McCoy made the most of his time off, holidaying in Barbados, getting married to Chanelle Burke in Mallorca a fortnight ago, and accepting an offer for his house that was too good to refuse, but the eleven-time champion is only really happy on the back of a horse and his relief to be back was palpable.

'I schooled twenty horses at Jackdaws Castle last week and it was like someone giving me a winning lottery ticket, that's how much it means to me,' he said. 'This is my life, and for me nothing compares to riding.

'I'm starting off again with everything to prove, that's the way I start every season. I'm lucky that I've been able to come back on levels with the rest and nobody's been able to get fifteen or twenty up on me, as that would take some catching.

'It's set up nicely, but it's still going to be hard work to be champion again – I'm certainly taking nothing for granted.'

McCoy said of claimer Tom O'Brien, who in the champion's absence had climbed to the top of the jockeys' table: 'I'm a great believer in statistics, and the stats tell you he's a good jockey.'

The season and the winners progressed to a twelfth championship, but two victories amongst the 184 were especially satisfying. They were both for Jonjo O'Neill, and the first was on an odd horse up against the son of an exceptional name. Jon Lees was the reporter.

THERE is no room for sentiment in the on-course make-up of Tony McCoy, whose unique brand of ruthlessness helped ensure the Pipe dream went up in smoke at Cheltenham yesterday.

McCOY'S SEASON 2006-2007	
wins:	184
rides:	758
strike rate:	24%
position in championship:	1st

Just when it looked as though Vodka Bleu would deliver an astonishing victory for fledgling trainer David Pipe in the Paddy Power Gold Cup, in which his father Martin was once dominant, McCoy extinguished all hope with a well-executed come-from-behind ride on the mercurial Exotic Dancer.

Of Pipe senior's seven winners in the previous ten runnings, McCoy was aboard three, but yesterday the champion jockey secured his first victory in the race since he severed full-time links with Pond House.

The victory had appeared particularly improbable because just five days earlier at Carlisle, Exotic Dancer had trailed Turpin Green by 28 lengths. Although that was his first run since fracturing a pelvis on Boxing Day last year, the performance did little to fill his rider with hope.

Yet, with trainer Jonjo O'Neill refitting cheekpieces for the first time in two seasons, McCoy found Exotic Dancer a much more willing partner as he made ground from three out to take control of the £110,000 prize from the final fence.

McCoy said: 'I thought a month ago he was the ideal horse for this race, but then he went to Carlisle and ran a shocker. He was too keen and there were three runners, but the most disappointing thing for me was that he didn't finish his race. The fact he didn't finish his race well meant you couldn't seriously fancy his chances here.

'I decided just to ride him today to get him round – if it all went wrong it would be my fault! I don't think it was a great ride – I think it just happened. He was more relaxed today.'

When Vodka Bleu and Taranis moved to the front with three to jump, the race looked set to be fought out between the first and second favourites, and then looked firmly within Pipe's grasp when the Paul Nicholls challenger came down at the next. But McCoy had still to play his hand and, after leading at the last, Exotic Dancer stretched to a three-length win over Vodka Bleu, who held New Alco for second with Butler's Cabin, stablemate of the winner, fourth.

Opposite: 'I don't think it was a great ride – I think it just happened': AP wins the Paddy Power Gold Cup at Cheltenham on Exotic Dancer, 11 November 2006.

O'Neill said: 'He's a funny old character. We've always thought he was a good horse but he hasn't produced it really, although he's run some good races in good-class races. He is frustrating.

'We went to Carlisle and thought he was going to run well, but it was a Mickey Mouse race really and he came back fresh and well so we decided to go. AP decided he was going to ride a waiting race but he still couldn't sit long enough.

'You don't know with this fellow. If he's on a going day you could fancy him but he hasn't had many going days. He wears ear plugs and they seemed to work. I think AP might be the key to him.'

The other great event for O'Neill and McCoy that season was a return to their native land and to a race which, surprisingly, neither of them had won before. Tony O'Hehir filed the report.

AP at Cheltenham on one of his favourite horses, Black Jack Ketchum.

BUTLER'S CABIN, who needed oxygen after winning at Cheltenham last month, showed his courage yet again to credit Tony McCoy and Jonjo O'Neill with their first Irish Grand National success.

The 14-1 shot, who was following up his National Hunt Chase success at the Festival, mastered fellow British raider Nine De Sivola by a length to land the €141,500 first prize.

Named after the place where Zach Johnson had been presented with the famous green jacket after winning the US Masters only 16 hours before, Butler's Cabin provided JP McManus, at home in Martinstown watching on television, with his second win in the race, 24 years after Bit Of A Skite, trained by Edward O'Grady, had won the big Easter Monday event.

The eighth British-trained winner of the race, Butler's Cabin again returned distressed. With the required oxygen supply sent to the third-last fence, where Cheeky Lady fell and sadly broke her back, water had to be used to revive the winner, whom O'Neill later reported to be 'fine'.

Surprisingly, O'Neill claimed to be paying his first visit to Fairyhouse: 'I never rode here, and though I've had a few runners here in the past, this is my first visit.'

McCoy was full of praise for O'Neill's achievement in having Butler's Cabin primed for yesterday's race. 'That was an unbelievable training performance, getting the horse back after the four-miler at Cheltenham where he collapsed after the race,' he said.

Reflecting on Butler's Cabin's victory, McCoy added: 'In big handicaps like today's race you need to have a horse who travels well and jumps well, and you also need to get a clear run. We got all three today and it has worked out very well.'

The phrase 'working out well' is never one to rely on in the jump racing firmament. So it was to prove come January when the ground came up to bite the champion.

For almost two months in early 2008, our McCoy reports became medical ones (and Gee Armytage, by the way, had become Gee Bradburne).

Overleaf: Fairyhouse, 9 April 2007: the Powers Whiskey Irish Grand National is in the bag as Butler's Cabin (left) takes the last fence ahead of Church Island, who finished fourth.

TONY McCOY was last night facing a race against time to be fit for the Cheltenham Festival after a crashing fall from the favourite Arnold Layne in the Totesport.com Classic Chase at Warwick yesterday.

McCoy was rushed for x-rays and assessment to University Hospital Walsgrave in Coventry, from where last night reports emerged that the twelve-time champion jockey had fractured two vertebrae at the base of his spine.

Were the injury to be as serious as reports indicated last night, McCoy could be sidelined for up to two months while he recovers and regains the proper level of fitness.

The report from the hospital last night was that McCoy was in a stable condition while his injuries were being fully assessed. A spokeswoman said: 'He's stable. He's still being assessed and looked at, but he is conscious and talking.

'When we asked him if we could give out a condition check he said, "Tell them I'm OK." But as yet we are not quite sure what his injuries are.'

McCoy came to grief from the 3-1 favourite Arnold Layne at the 14th fence. Racegoers and television viewers watched as the rider lay prone on the track but was quickly attended to by medical personnel. He was fitted with a neck brace before being carefully loaded into a waiting ambulance, after which he was taken to hospital for x-rays on his lower back.

Jonjo O'Neill, to whose stable McCoy is attached through his retainer with JP McManus, witnessed the fall. He said: 'It was bad enough, but Tony got a pretty good kicking as well, and he's got a lot of pain from both sides of his lower back.

'However, he was moving his legs all right and he's so tough that you can guarantee he won't be out of action for a second longer than necessary.'

TONY McCOY yesterday underwent surgery which it is hoped will guarantee him being fit for the Cheltenham Festival in March.

The extent of the perennial champion jockey's injuries following his crashing fall at Warwick last Saturday had been finally established earlier in the day after he was seen by two of Britain's leading spinal specialists at Nuffield Hospital in Oxford.

While it had previously been reported that McCoy had suffered a fracture of the T12 vertebra, the 33-year-old was hoping an MRI scan would reveal nothing worse than severe bruising when he was transferred on Monday night from the hospital in Coventry, where he was taken after sustaining the injury partnering Arnold Layne in the Totesport.com Classic Chase.

Speaking yesterday afternoon, McCoy's assistant Gee Bradburne said: 'James Wilson-MacDonald and Jeremy Fairbank looked at the MRI scan, and it suggested there was a small piece of loose bone off the vertebra and that can easily be fixed with a small operation, which they are doing now.

'This will speed up recovery and guarantee him back for Cheltenham.

Albertas Run in full flight on the way to winning the Dalepak Beginners' Chase at Towcester, 10 October 2007.

'They just think that by stabilising that, they are going to be in a better position to carry on. If you don't stabilise it, you have to lie on your back for ages – I know this from my own experience, you have to lie on your back with braces and God knows what – but once Tony is stabilised, he can come home. Then they encourage movement, and away you go, really.'

Bradburne expects McCoy to remain in hospital for a couple of days and, knowing her employer's temperament, admitted she would be surprised if it proved any longer.

Bradburne dismissed the two broken ribs McCoy has also sustained as 'neither here nor there, those will be all right.'

She added: 'The CT scans and x-rays don't show nearly as much as the MRI, and these guys, obviously being the top spinal specialists, decided to do an MRI scan to check it all out, and that is what they have come up with.'

ONLY ONE week after sustaining a serious spinal injury in a fall at Warwick, the seemingly indestructible Tony McCoy walked out of the John Radcliffe Hospital in Oxford yesterday to begin an all-important six weeks of recuperation before returning to the saddle.

The fact that the champion jockey was leaving his hospital bed just four days after an operation to repair the damage to his T12 vertebra – and 24 hours ahead of schedule – speaks volumes for his resilience and will to win the battle ahead.

With the prestigious Cheltenham Festival looming on jump racing's horizon in seven weeks, it initially looked to be a race against time for McCoy to recover fully, but he now thinks he will comfortably beat the deadline and be back riding at the beginning of March.

Speaking before leaving hospital yesterday, he said: 'It will be good to get home to Lambourn to be with my family, as I've been flat out in bed for much of the last week. But I must be a good healer as it's hard to believe the progress I've made since the operation on Tuesday.

'Dr James Wilson-MacDonald came in this morning, saw me walking around and was so amazed that I'd become so mobile already that he immediately told me I could leave the hospital this afternoon.'

However, McCoy is all too well aware that, taking into account the seriousness of the injury, he will not be trying to rush the recovery and return too quickly to his day job.

'It was obviously not a normal injury and I'm going to have to do all the right things and take notice of what the specialists tell me, as my back is the engine room to my whole body and there will be no returning until things are 100 per cent,' he added.

Asked if the fact that he was now a father had altered his outlook when taking falls, he replied: 'Not really. Just because I'm a dad now doesn't mean I'm not going to have falls in races, as that is part and parcel of my job.

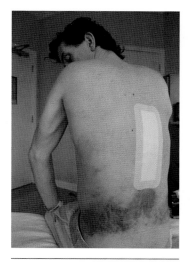

Battered and bruised.

'When you have a fall there is always a chance you're going to get injured. It's something all jockeys have to live with every time they go out to get on a horse and compete, and we all have to accept that.

'I'm a shocking patient. I know injury is part of the game – in England and Ireland this year, I'll have had 600 rides already and you're obviously going to get falls. It's part of the job. If you don't expect it you're in the wrong game.'

McCoy's recollections remain lucid of his fall from Arnold Layne at Warwick eight days ago that resulted in his being taken to hospital in Coventry, before a switch to the John Radcliffe for the operation.

He said: 'It was one of those falls that didn't seem bad but I landed awkwardly and was struggling to get up and down, so I guessed at the time I had not taken the normal kick you can get when this sort of thing happens.

'Also, I was finding my breathing was not right, but the doctors and paramedics at Warwick were first-class and I cannot thank them enough for everything they did, though I was never in that much pain.

'Even after the operation I was not on painkillers, so I guess that might be a good omen for me making a quick and full recovery and the first week of March or something like that could see me back riding.'

While in hospital McCoy's spirits have been kept high by visits from the likes of Jonjo O'Neill, Mick Fitzgerald, Carl Llewellyn, Jimmy McCarthy, Dominic Elsworth and Paddy Brennan, and by a host of messages from many other well-wishers.

'I'd like to say thank you to all the people who have been in touch,' he added. 'But the biggest thank you of all has to go to Dr Philip Pritchard, who has been a rock all through this unfortunate episode.

'He arranged for me to be transferred to the hospital in Oxford and that I saw Dr Wilson-MacDonald and Abi Zubovic, who carried out the operation that sees me set off on the road to recovery a lot faster than seemed probable in the ambulance taking me to hospital from Warwick last Saturday.

'Philip, thanks for everything and I will, hopefully, be seeing you back on the racecourse soon!'

TONY McCOY could undergo kriotherapy treatment in a fortnight's time to aid his quest to return to race-riding in early March.

The champion jockey left John Radcliffe Hospital in Oxford eleven days ago, a week after sustaining back injuries when Arnold Layne fell at Warwick, and has underlined his determination to make a full recovery in the build-up to the Cheltenham Festival.

The revolutionary kriotherapy treatment, which helps speed rehabilitation, involves spending a few minutes in an ice chamber being blasted with liquid nitrogen at temperatures well below −100°C.

It was instrumental in helping Ryan Moore make an early return to action from a broken right elbow sustained at Lingfield last March.

McCoy is convalescing at home in Lambourn but, typically, is not proving the best of patients and will visit his doctor shortly to determine whether he can undergo the kriotherapy treatment.

McCoy said: 'Physically, I feel fine and I'm getting around very easily, but mentally I'm finding it frustrating.

'I have to speak to the doctor again first but I could have the treatment in two weeks' time.

'It obviously depends at what stage my back problem is, and I will be doing everything he tells me to.

'Basically, when I'm given the go-ahead to step up, then I can have the treatment.'

The 2008 Cheltenham Festival was due to start on 11 March, and it was only on the 8th that we saw McCoy on the racetrack again. It was a welcome sight.

HE had been insisting for nearly two weeks that he was fit to resume, and yesterday Tony McCoy provided public confirmation of his recovery from two fractured vertebrae when his eagerly awaited comeback passed without incident at Sandown.

Easing his way back eight weeks after the fall from Arnold Layne at Warwick with two mounts over hurdles, the champion jockey finished fifth on Rapid Increase and a never-threatening 13th on the JP McManus-owned Tarlac in the Sunderlands Imperial Cup.

Hearts were almost in mouths when Rapid Increase hit the last hurdle in the opener, but McCoy was typically unfazed and walked back to the weighing room barely out of breath.

'I wasn't on the best horse, but it was grand,' he said. 'I feel good, but I'm just happy to be back riding, to be honest. I was getting very frustrated sat at home watching everybody else. I'll obviously be happier when I can ride a few winners.

'I had a good recovery, but I wouldn't be doing this if I wasn't fit. I'm not just coming back to make up the numbers. It's good to have the ride, but I was pretty fit.'

McCoy is booked for two rides at Hereford today and will then focus on the Cheltenham Festival, the prime motivation behind his determination to come back.

'It was pretty depressing the first couple of weeks because I was just lying on my back, getting a bit fat, but then I was in Dubai for ten days, which was good,' he said.

'I was walking along the beach for five or six miles every day in the sun, which helped. Then I was at Champneys Health Spa for ten days and had kriotherapy and plenty of exercise to help me get fit.

'The last two weeks I have been back riding out every day. Cheltenham was a massive motivation, but I would do the same thing even if Cheltenham wasn't on and it was the middle of summer.'

Victory on Albertas Run in the Festival's Royal & SunAlliance Chase made most of those privations worth it, but the true compensation was once again sought at Aintree.

It would be McCoy's thirteenth tilt at the Grand National. Butler's Cabin was the chosen conveyance, but when Peter Thomas went along the week before, he found himself thinking as much of AP's recovery as of hopes of an Aintree rekindling.

THERE WAS something faintly unsettling about all those pictures of AP McCoy emerging from the kriotherapy chamber after yet another brutal phase of his rehabilitation from spinal injury. Yes, he was cold and distressed, as you would expect of a man plunged into inhumanly low temperatures for inhumanly long spells. But there was something else there, an unnerving look that was equal parts pain and triumphal pleasure.

As a steady stream of ill-advised, puny journalists tottered out of the torture room, having accompanied him halfway to his physical limits, the champion jockey followed them, looking as though he had simply been sitting in a chilly church hall without his duffel coat on. Left to his own devices, with the dial turned down to a primeval −135°C, he stepped into the doorway, framed by a cloud of white light and liquid nitrogen, like an avenging hero come to reclaim his birthright.

On the long, hollow face, there was a blue-lipped smile that spoke of another small but significant victory. Had his mouth not been frozen in that grin, he would surely have tilted his head to the heavens and bellowed: 'Robert Falcon Scott, Sir Ernest Shackleton,

Roald Amundsen, Richard Dunwoody, can you hear me? You boys took a hell of a beating!'

Now, however, McCoy is sitting hunched in the corner of a changing room at an inclement racecourse, and although the conditions are far less barbaric than in kriotherapy, the satisfaction levels have plummeted accordingly. His 13th consecutive jockeys' title is all but in the bag despite his two months on the sick list, but today is not going well.

For most of us, such a rapid comeback from injury would be achievement enough for one season, and it was clearly a feat that invigorated McCoy immensely. But that was then.

Achievement for the champion is measured not by the year or by the day but by the winner, and today will yield none, so he is a failure. His shifting, frustrated demeanour suggests he would be happier back in the deep freeze.

'The cold wasn't that bad,' he says, almost wistfully.

'Rehab isn't that bad if it's working. If it's making you better, you like doing it. All I wanted to do was work myself to death and get back riding as soon as I could.

'It's not about the pain. The worst injuries are the ones that take longest to come back from. They're the ones that hurt the most.'

McCoy's latest struggle with the accepted limits of the human condition began officially on 12 January at Warwick, when he was dumped by a horse called Arnold Layne, although he is convinced the roots of the problem stretch back to another fall at Lingfield in November. What is beyond doubt is that he left Oxford's John Radcliffe hospital characteristically ahead of schedule, with metal plates where once there were only damaged vertebrae, and that his current efforts are not without their accompanying discomforts. The broken ribs, forgotten in the blaze of kriotherapic publicity and dismissed by his assistant, Gee Bradburne, as 'neither here nor there', healed quickly, but the big injury lingered.

'I was as good as you could expect,' says the 33-year-old.

'When I got out of the car, I felt stiff, and it was like that for a while, but after a bit of exercise it was fine. It was muscle pain more than anything else, muscle damage where they cut through to put the plates in, and it took a while to get better. I'll have the plates out in the summer.'

Despite a Cheltenham Festival winner on Albertas Run for Jonjo O'Neill that must have acted as a galvanising relief for both men, there's a sense that top gear has yet to be re-engaged.

'Winners and quality of rides have not been great since I came back,' confides the champ, 'but I've only been having a couple of rides each day, and I haven't been beaten on any that I came back thinking I'd have won on three months ago.'

If McCoy ever wished for the ultimate test of his recuperative powers he will be regretting it now, in the thick of the most gruelling challenge of his professional year – the annual barrage of enquiries concerning his failure to win 'the nation's favourite race'. He will need to be at his peak to withstand such an onslaught, although by now he must be getting used to it.

Have you been unlucky?

Would Clan Royal have won?

How did you get beat on Blowing Wind?

Which one will you be on this year? Are you sure that's the right one? Can't you ride Aintree? Have you gone at the game? Why don't you ask Mick Fitzgerald?

'It's nice that people still think you should have won it,' he says, indulgently. 'There's lots of people have won the Grand National that I don't know how they won it, but they did – Marcus Armytage, Gee's brother, being one of them.

'It's annoying, of course, but it's not the easiest thing in the world to do. You need a lot of luck, you need to get on the right horse, and even when you think you're on the right horse, like I did with Blowing Wind, it doesn't mean you're going to win it.

'I've ridden horses that I didn't fancy at all and got good rides off them. I thought Challenger Du Luc was tailor-made for it but he head-butted the first fence – it was like he was on a suicide mission. You never know until you get out there.'

This year, McCoy is hoping Butler's Cabin will be the horse to break his duck in the famous green and gold hoops of JP McManus.

> 'There's lots of people have won the Grand National that I don't know how they've won it, but they did.'
>
> TONY McCOY

The eight-year-old goes into the race a proven stayer, having won both the four-miler at Cheltenham and the Irish Grand National last year, but although the champ remains ever hopeful, full-tilt optimism seems in short supply.

'He has a tried-and-tested look to him in stamina terms,' says McCoy. 'Horses with 11st or more have it tough, but the compressed handicap should help in that respect.

'I was quite happy with him first time up this season, third to Jack The Giant over 2m4f at Leicester. He got outpaced and then stayed on well from the last, but he must have been disappointing since then – last of seven at Sandown and third, beaten 54 lengths, at Wincanton.

'This has been his goal all season, though, and while you would like him to have shown a little more spark in his last two races, Saturday is D-Day for him and you'd hope he'd go there in his best form of the year and redeem himself. I think he deserves my faith.

'I schooled him last week and he jumps pretty well. I didn't see any reason not to be riding him. There was no negative vibe at all.'

Of course, the only one to judge McCoy's career by his failure to win the Grand National would be McCoy himself. The history books and the racing public will be a little more forgiving, whatever the eventual result of the tussle between AP and the big spruce fences, but there's no sign that his need to win everything is being diluted by his success at winning most things.

He's tried getting married, having a baby and talking to his therapist, John Francome, but still he can't shake off the black dog that is his compulsion not to be beaten.

'No, family life hasn't changed my outlook to racing,' he admits. 'I'm not more cautious about which horses I ride, although maybe my agent is, and I still pick at things in my mind when perhaps I'd be happier if I could let them go. But while I'm still riding there's no way I can. There has to be a reason for doing what I do and I can't just go through the motions.

'The thing about Chanelle and me is that we've been together a long time, and she knows what I'm like and she knows when things are not going right. Some people might take it to heart and think it's their fault, but she just doesn't ask. She doesn't try to find out what's wrong, because she already knows what's wrong.

'She says she knows from the sound of me putting my keys down when I come through the door whether it's good or bad. She doesn't have to look at the results. At the end of the day, as long as I come home, she's happy.'

McCoy says he's happy, too.

Happy with the way he's riding and enjoying what he's doing, with the proviso that he can be miserable about it when he wants to be. Victory in the big 'un on Saturday would bring about a deep-seated joy, and no mistake, but what's the betting it would only last until the next loser?

So Butler's Cabin would be the thirteenth to carry the Grand National banner. In two pithy post-race paragraphs, Lee Mottershead explained why it was not to prove a lucky number.

THIRTEEN was not Tony McCoy's lucky number. On his 13th Grand National ride, the champion jockey was sat a close fifth on Butler's Cabin, travelling strongly and not more than a length off the lead, when the horse knuckled over on landing at the second Becher's Brook and exited the race.

'I was having a good ride. He was travelling nicely but just tipped up at Becher's,' said McCoy, while the horse's trainer Jonjo O'Neill – also still without a Grand National triumph – took the reverse in good humour. He said: 'The horse is all right and Tony has been good about it as well, but that's because we're getting used to this happening!'

It may have been a 13th Grand National failure, but on 13 April we were reporting a first winner in the Queen's colours, on Barber's Shop at Newbury the day before, and at the season's close at Sandown AP was celebrating a 13th consecutive jockeys' title.

> 'The horse is all right and Tony has been good about it as well, but that's because we're getting used to this happening!'
>
> JONJO O'NEILL

185

John Smith's Grand National, 5 April 2008: another National dream disappears as Butler's Cabin crumples at Becher's Brook second time round.

DESPITE being the first jockey since Fred Archer more than 100 years ago to be crowned champion for a 13th consecutive season, Tony McCoy was yesterday keen to put the campaign behind him.

An injury-hit season meant that McCoy's tally of 140 wins was his lowest since he was a conditional in 1994-95 and, with no wins in the championship races at the Cheltenham Festival and a first Grand National success still elusive, McCoy, who was at Punchestown yesterday – his wife Chanelle and young daughter Eve collected his prize at Sandown – was far from celebrating.

The perennial champion jockey, who will head to Ludlow today to start the defence of his title, said: 'Even apart from my back injury it has been a frustrating season. It's always nice to be champion, but it definitely wasn't my best year.'

McCoy's wife spoke of her astonishment at her husband's mental strength to return from breaking two vertebrae in a fall in January in time to make the Cheltenham Festival.

'He did superbly to come back from the back injury,' she said. 'I think Eve kept him going and kept his spirits alive. The treatment he had was extreme and it was unbelievable to see someone with such mental strength.

'When he was told by the doctor he wasn't going to be able to ride at Cheltenham, he just didn't accept it. He's also grateful to be able to count on the help of people like Mr McManus, Jonjo O'Neill and Charles Egerton.'

Comparisons with Fred Archer, the last jockey to win 13 consecutive titles, are not entirely happy ones. He too was a tall and courteous man in private but a tiger on the track. But for him the pressure of wasting so tipped him into madness that he shot himself at only 29. In 2008 McCoy was already 33. The pressures and the winning addiction remained, and Grand National fulfilment remained the lure.

McCOY'S SEASON 2007-2008	
wins:	140
rides:	648
strike rate:	22%
position in championship:	1st

FULFILMENT

Everyone knows how this section ends, because everyone saw the 2010 Grand National finish and the climactic moments afterwards when McCoy let all the glory roar. In hindsight, the 17 months linking Master Minded winning the Tingle Creek Chase in December 2008 and the symbolically named Don't Push It ending 15 years of National hurt in April 2010 have an inevitability about them. But, McCoy being McCoy, there was plenty of drama along the way.

On Master Minded he was being used as a super-super-sub to take the pressure off Paul Nicholls' stable jockey Sam Thomas, who had been unseated by top horses Kauto Star at Haydock and Big Buck's at Newbury on consecutive Saturdays.

McCoy, of course, offers rather more than just a 'safe pair of hands'. Alastair Down was at Sandown to appreciate it.

MANY seasons ago something akin to an unbreakable contract grew up between the betting public and AP McCoy.

If he never changed, they would never waver in their support of the greatest single ally they have ever had on their side.

AP isn't infallible but he is most definitely unquenchable, and that fiendish compulsion not to get beat still leaves him in a place only he inhabits – somewhere between deserving a medal and being a suitable case for locking up.

The public love him because he has never abused their trust, never let them down.

Blazingly honest in a game of partial truths and institutionalised chicanery, he is driven by one thing – the scent of the next winner.

Last Saturday he rattled off four winners at Newbury, and his first reaction was to bemoan the fact that the Hennessy was not among them. Time was when I might have thought 'miserable so-and-so', but that is to miss the point. If AP didn't think like that he wouldn't be the totemic life force that he has become year-on-gruelling-injury-mashed-year.

Yesterday he netted four more and this time, courtesy of Master Minded in the Tingle Creek, the big race did not escape the mesh of his winner-trawling net.

Previous spread: John Smith's Grand National, 10 April 2010: AP and Don't Push It (left) head Denis O'Regan on Black Apalachi at the last fence, with Barry Geraghty on Big Fella Thanks, who finished fourth, on the right.

Master Minded was in exhibition mood, and those who had been questioning his jumping found there wasn't even a case to answer round this trappiest of courses.

Despite the risk-charged imponderable of first-fence wipe-out loose horse Fieppes Shuffle dogging him all the way, Master Minded jumped flawlessly whereas his principal rivals blundered their chances into oblivion.

Paul Nicholls' eyebrows went heavenward at the suggestion that Master Minded has any sort of jumping issue, and word reaches me that after questions about his fencing were raised on yesterday's *Morning Line* the series of loud explosions heard from Ireland could be traced to an incredulous Ruby Walsh, who wondered whether the pundits were talking about the same horse on which he won the Champion Chase.

Nicholls and Walsh are understandably loyal to their stars, but they have a point. It is the job of the press and other racing pundits to analyse and question the performances of both horses and riders. But am I alone in having the sneaking feeling that we are

AP and Master Minded at the second last ahead of Twist Magic – who is about to fall – in the Seasons Holidays Tingle Creek Chase at Sandown Park, 6 December 2008.

'Every day is a pressure day.'

TONY McCOY

getting a touch obsessive in trying to impose on various half-ton creatures some pattern of perfection that a lot of them don't wear easily?

Some of the recent comment on Kauto Star and Master Minded has teetered on the edge of the plain silly. The need for journalists to report the news is our paramount duty, but there is all the difference in the world between dispassionate treatment of a horse or jockey's possible shortcomings and the increasing fashion for making a life or death issue out of something that may not even be there.

The racing public are not stupid. They know that jump racing generates a throbbing atmosphere and spectacular excitement.

They also know that you cannot artificially whip up either of those priceless qualities.

There is no point in keeping a boiling kettle on the gas – it won't get any hotter.

As AP returned on Master Minded he deflected a question about pressure in the build-up to the race with the remark that 'every day is a pressure day.' My gut feeling is that AP couldn't give a flying one about any pressure imposed on him from outside.

The only pressure to which he responds comes from inside himself, which makes McCoy such a very singular and extreme sporting figure.

He closed out his day with a typical grind on Kilbeggan Blade, who took the London National for the second year running. Last season it was Paddy Brennan in the saddle, this time AP – two men who think 'de feet' is something on which you put 'de shoes'.

I bet Kilbeggan Blade won't load at Tom George's for a third crack this time next year without some guarantee from the trainer that he has found a normal human being to do the steering this time.

McCoy would have ridden five winners but for a mind-boggling performance by Choc Thornton and Araldur, who stuck on harder than Araldite to deny Free World in the Henry VIII Novices' Chase.

When Free World winged the Pond fence it looked all over and

Araldur's supporters needed St Jude, the patron saint of lost causes.

But in St Jude's absence Thornton proved a more than adequate substitute. He never stopped galvanising Araldur, who responded with utmost gameness to every kitchen sink that came his way to stretch out his long neck and mug the favourite close home.

Thornton made much of the fact that Araldur was the most willing of partners, but there is no need to be modest about this ride – it was an absolute belter, a classic confrontation between two men at the very top of their dangerous games.

This result will have saved bookmakers fortunes, although the McCoy four-timer will still mean that in betting shops up and down the land many a small punter's multiple will burn the fingers of the settlers' hands. The fact that he rode four on Hennessy day won't have stopped the faithful winging in again behind their man a week later – why ever doubt that the incredible can achieve the improbable?

In an already fizzing jumps season this was a marvellous Tingle Creek afternoon. Master Minded reminded us just why the superlatives flowed so free back in March and AP, pale as ever but as lethal as usual, was king of this Sandown hill, as he has long been king of so many others.

As the winners flowed, so another impossible milestone, that of 3,000 winners over jumps in Britain and Ireland, loomed swiftly on the horizon. Reaching it was time to reflect again on the private man behind the public face, but before reading Alastair Down's eve-of-tri-millennium interview, it's worth taking the evidence of someone who sees the private side every day, AP's wife Chanelle.

Under the headline 'Behind Every Great Man …', Rodney Masters had an illuminating interview with her in January 2009.

AND now, the Tony McCoy the public has never seen.

Courtesy of Mrs Chanelle McCoy, who has known and loved him for 13 years, and the adorably cute Miss Eve McCoy, aged 15 months.

In the lounge of their Lambourn home, blessed with surely the most stunning panoramic view in Berkshire, Chanelle is detailing startling evidence of her husband's superhuman depths of willpower and sacrifice.

On a lighter note, she tells of his ability to faultlessly recite scripts from *Only Fools and Horses*, a show he watches most nights before bedtime on either UK Gold or a DVD. Also of his acute wit, and – the most betraying factor in every household – on whose armchair rests the television remote control.

His dislikes are few, but Chanelle divulges the number one. To her bewilderment, and occasional embarrassment, he detests service stations where payment is made via the 'late night' window, necessitating shoppers to point out to the cashier the items they want to purchase. She says he'd rather drive to another outlet, and frequently will do so, if the petrol gauge has nudged zero.

Meanwhile, from an adjacent room there emits a noisy symphony of male and female chortling. McCoy is playing with Eve, both of them immersed in a sea of toys. An illustration of his devotion as a family man came at the end of last week when, although riding at Doncaster on Friday and Saturday, he made his way home after the first day, with a 330-mile round trip, to be with his wife and daughter, who had spent most of that week in Ireland.

Those who witness the austere, deadpan character in work mode on the racecourse will be surprised, but the McCoy home is undoubtedly a house full of fun. 'I appreciate the public see little evidence of that, but Anthony is actually very amusing,' says Chanelle. 'He'll often have me in stitches. I think he gets that from his mother, who has a super sense of humour.'

His public persona is indeed a topic discussed by the couple on occasions.

She says: 'Over the years, I've challenged Anthony that the public are getting a wrong perception of him, and he'll ask if I walk round my office all day smiling from ear to ear.

'On the other hand, when he's watching his race replays in the evening and an interview with him pops up, where he has been quite stern, I'd then diplomatically point out that if he was a member of the public watching, what would he think? He'd reply that his thoughts are invariably focused on the next ride, but he'd concede that yes, maybe he can be rather difficult to interview and come across as too serious. But that's water off a duck's back to him. I do understand because a lot of us are different characters in our work environment.'

However, his overall character has changed, and for the better, since they first met at the Punchestown festival in 1996. She was a 19-year-old at college and, though not particularly consumed by racing, had organised a visit there by 30 fellow students. 'At college, if you organised a society, Guinness would sponsor it and give you free days out!' They were introduced by mutual friend Anna Moore, daughter of trainer Arthur Moore. Anna had described McCoy as this young bucko over from England who may be willing to give a talk to the group.

'I can't say it was an instant attraction for me,' Chanelle remembers. 'Anthony would ring up and we'd chat away. The more we spoke, the more I liked him. Over the next six months he grew on me. In our early days of dating we broke up more than once. I think the problem was that he was unable to balance his obsession with his job and maintain a relationship at the same time.

'In his early twenties he was really miserable at times, unhappy in himself, unhappy with life. I think for people who achieve a lot at such a young age there's a fear of not being able to maintain it, a fear that they'll be a one-year, perhaps two-year, wonder, then fade away. Sometimes it's considerably tougher to stay at the top than it was to get there.

'In those days we'd talk for hours about why he wasn't happy. When we'd break up he'd ask me how, when he wasn't happy within himself, could he make me happy? I knew he loved me, but he struggled to cope with the two aspects of life.

'But around the age of 25 he became more content, a better balanced personality. It was nothing sudden, and happened over a two-year period, in his final year with Mr Pipe, and his first with Mr McManus.'

After so many championship titles, what drives him on? The clue is on the coffee table before us. One of his first trophies. 'It's a numbers game for Anthony, and not related to prize-money,' says Chanelle. 'My view is that he's driven by the fear of not being champion. It means so much to him. He's as enthusiastic about race-riding now as he was when I first met him.'

And with his success comes a gruelling regime. 'I'm so utterly proud of him. I wonder from where he summons up so much energy. He is incredibly strong. He has to control his weight and that takes enormous mental strength, yet never once has he complained. There are nights he'll come home from the races and spend two hours in the bath. He'd reckon to lose 4lb per hour. He'll come out with his skin like a prune. I've seen him sitting on the bathroom floor, utterly whacked.

'Early on in his career he was on a bad diet, mainly Kit Kats and Diet Coke, but now he's more sensible, and he'll take plenty of vitamins. It remains a struggle. For instance, he rang the other day and asked me to cook a piece of chicken for dinner because he hadn't eaten for a day and a half and he was starving. A short while later he rang back and told me not to bother with the chicken because he'd spoken to Dave Roberts, his agent, and was doing light the next day. That night he made do with a cup of tea before spending two hours in the bath.

'He has such incredible mental willpower. He's ticklish, but if I tickle him when we're in bed he can engage a state of mind where he's frozen and will not laugh. I'll ask him how he does it, and he'll say, "It's a mental thing Chanelle, a power of the mind." Then he'll tickle me, and teach me how to cope in the same way.

'He has this belief that nothing can beat you mentally unless you allow it. I often wonder from where that emanated. Possibly during his time with Jim Bolger, who had a great influence on Anthony's work ethic.'

The McCoy home has ten televisions. As Chanelle much prefers to read, her husband's choice of viewing goes unchallenged when they are on the sofa together. They have a strict pact that they will not watch television during the half-hour of their evening meal at 7pm so they can catch up on each other's day.

There's never a dearth of topics to talk about. Chanelle is a successful businesswoman, working up to ten hours a day, five days a week, and she travels abroad for four months every year. She is a business development director at her parents' pharmaceutical company, which is based in Ireland and serves 80 countries. She is responsible for western Europe and the Middle East.

'Tony is always interested in what's happening in my job, on how many contracts I've signed. I think it gives him a degree of escapism,' she says.

They were granted planning permission last month for a 60-box yard on their estate. McCoy remains adamant that he will rent them out, and never train himself, but does his wife consider there will be a change of heart once he quits race-riding?

'We've not discussed when he might retire, but I'm sure he won't ride on for too long. I've never asked him what he plans to do next, but it's sure to be something mentally stimulating.

'It would be impossible to be as successful as he has been twice in a lifetime, and I would hate him to believe he had to be the very best in whatever profession he turns to.'

When asked what alternative career path her husband would have pursued had he not been a jockey, she bursts into laughter. 'I can't possibly tell you.' Persuaded to do her best, she pops next door and says to her husband: 'Anthony, should I tell him?'

He agrees. The answer is an assassin, a Jason Bourne-type secret agent. 'He idolises Jason and reckons he'd be very good at his job. I kid you not.'

CHANELLE McCOY ON …

Her husband's adjustment to fatherhood

'It hasn't changed Anthony because he has always been lovely to live with and, contrary to the myth out there, is an easy-going character. He's a super dad and adores playing with Eve.

'She's definitely a McCoy, and I've a feeling she'll be the competitive type because before she was walking her father was guiding her on a walker, and now she's walking he's teaching her to run! Anthony is a family man. He idolises his mother and father, and his four sisters and brother. I'm lucky to have such lovely in-laws.'

Life in the woods

'We've 40 acres of woodland and Anthony spends hours there cutting logs for the house. As he was always moaning to me about a blunt axe, I bought him a chainsaw for Christmas, and a pair of chainsaw-proof trousers – we have to keep those legs safe! He loves it, and there's now a nine-month store of logs.'

That fall at Warwick in January 2008

'I was in London with Eve. I knew something was wrong when I saw Jonjo's wife Jacqui O'Neill's name come up on my phone.

I dropped off Eve with Gee Bradburne, and headed for the hospital. I felt so sorry for him. People would ask me if I was all right, but all my thoughts were with Anthony. He has taught me to be a no-nonsense person. He amazed the doctors by his utter determination to make a speedy recovery – another example of his extraordinary mental strength.'

Clothes

'I buy them for him. Ruby Walsh, who stays with us a lot – he's the perfect house guest because he makes his bed and washes up his tea mug – is always teasing Anthony about his shirts and ties, but I've noticed recently that Ruby is getting more flash and adventurous with his clothes.'

The chores

'I'll cook dinner, and Anthony will clear the table and load the dishwasher. When I was expecting Eve, he would do the weekly shop at Tesco in Newbury. We're a Tesco family. Waitrose is too flash for us. We mind the pennies.'

The toothpaste

'He does squeeze the tube in the wrong place, but he never irritates me by that or anything else he does. On very rare occasions he can make me cross, but he'll never grate on me.'

Who's the boss?

'Definitely Anthony, no question. But I'm the organiser. I book everything.'

The headline on Alastair Down's piece was 'First Among Equals'.

AN ESSENTIALLY private man is in a very public place this week as some obscure horse, name unknown, moves closer to becoming immortalised in the wisdom of anoraks as the animal on which Tony McCoy rode winner number 3,000.

> 'He amazed the doctors by his utter determination to make a speedy recovery – another example of his extraordinary mental strength.'
>
> CHANELLE McCOY

The fact that you could walk McCoy three times round Trafalgar Square without him being recognised sits hard with many racing fans, who see men of lesser fibre and a fraction of his achievement lauded like gods or set up as heroes that they are palpably not. But we shouldn't be exercised by the phenomenon of McCoy being lost on the public at large, because while he wants recognition and acknowledgement, one of the things that sets him apart is that he doesn't crave it. Except perhaps from himself.

Last week, on a blank day, there was only one untidy and mucky thing cluttering up the immaculate marble-topped kitchen in the McCoy house and that was the jockey himself who, with the light gone, had hauled his spare frame in from outside, covered in paint. On the wall-mounted television, President Obama was being sworn in stutteringly, and in his hilltop lair just outside Lambourn McCoy settled down with his mug of tea – another man whose achievements mark him out as being of a very different stripe to all who have gone before.

Affable and polite, he is not a smiley man, and the thing that has always struck me about him is that ten per cent of him is always somewhere else, dwelling on anything from the price of emulsion, the result of the Arsenal game, or whether some yak at Jonjo's has learned to jump yet.

His friend, rival and lodger Ruby Walsh sees the disconnection and says: 'It is his mindset. When he passes the post in a race he is not thinking about the race that has gone or the moment, he is already asking himself "Where is this horse going next? Where is it going to win next?"'

Walsh, who spends seven or eight nights a month at McCoy's in what his host laughingly refers to as the Ruby Suite, adds: 'He is quiet enough with that droll old face of his – until he gets rattled. If someone does something stupid or out of order in the weighing room he wouldn't put up with it. He'd be the first to step in to stop a fight if a couple of the young fellers thought they were going to start one. He is no shrinking violet.

'But he is great company and has a terrific sense of humour. You never catch him strutting around doing the "I'm the champion" thing, and while he may not drink, often as not he is the last to go home if there is a big night out. Some evenings you walk into his house and you can hear him upstairs playing with Eve and just howling with laughter.

'I tell you, he has made riding in Britain easy for me.'

Sometimes figures and statistics get so out of hand that they can lose their impact. The number 3,000 has been waved around so much in recent days that we have begun to get blasé about it.

Just six years ago, McCoy became the winningmost jump jockey of all time when overhauling Richard Dunwoody by riding his 1,700th winner, and we all shook our heads and thought we would never see the like of it again. Well, we are going to, because he is well on his way to doubling that figure and becoming the man who has ridden twice as many winners as anyone else.

And as he has amassed that incredible haul, two things have bound the racing public to him. First, we appreciate the priceless truth that he tries heart and soul every time he throws a battered leg across one, and second, we have seen the personal torment involved in the process. Watching him in the moments of disappointment and anger has given us all some tiny idea of the places he has taken himself in order to get to the place he is.

This is a man who starts most days with an hour in a bath that is almost hot enough to boil an egg, and definitely hot enough to waste a McCoy. When he says, 'I can remember days when I have lain on the bathroom floor almost in tears,' he is telling you that you can edit out the 'almost'.

He says: 'I don't think I have become any mellower, but I have learned how to cope and to handle things better. The weighing room is a fantastic place but a very tough one because out on the course you have no friends, it is all about beating them. Yet there we all are getting changed together – and I don't think Manchester United get changed with the opposition before a big match.

'You see some young lads come in who think they can't be bothered with the way things are done, but they all come round to the same way of thinking in time, and you will never find better

> 'I don't think I have become any mellower, but I have learned how to cope and to handle things better.'
>
> TONY McCOY

Three legends of the sport: Lester Piggott, Jonjo O'Neill and AP at Cheltenham.

company than in there. You hear the funniest stories, and if you sit next to Warren Marston as I do you laugh so much sometimes that you could burst.'

McCoy himself laughs at a couple of low points in his spectacularly successful association with Martin Pipe and remembers: 'We had two rows and neither were to do with my riding. The first was when I had been injured and the owner wanted Norman Williamson to stay on one he had been riding. It was a fairly sharp disagreement and I was 100 per cent right!

'The other was when I was beat a short head on Rodock by Pipey's other runner Copeland in a big handicap hurdle at Sandown. I went absolutely ballistic and we didn't speak for two weeks. But he was a great man to ride for and I tell you he will never get the credit he deserves for what he did for horses and their welfare.

'Nobody ever did more for horses' fitness and health and I feel privileged to have been a part of it.'

But even in those great days there were times you sensed he was paying prices that others were not. I shall never forget seeing him hurl his whip into the crowd when returning in angry triumph on Cyfor Malta after the 1998 Murphy's Gold Cup at Cheltenham. Beleaguered by the whip rules and seemingly convinced the authorities had an agenda against him, he had the air of a hunted man and the thought arose, 'Nobody can go on like this.'

Then there have been the festivals that have turned sour on him and he on them. The most telling moment came when, winnerless and making an exhibition of himself that was painful to watch, he found the figure of Ted Walsh standing by him in the weighing room. At the time, his first and much-loved mentor Billy Rock was dying in Ireland, and Ted asked him: 'How are you going?'

The reply came unsmilingly along the lines of 'Not too well', to which Ted delivered the devastating riposte 'Well, you are going a hell of a lot better than Billy Rock' before turning on his heel.

Some would judge it a cruel remark, but it was anything but. I can just see Ted's frustration exploding out of him at the sight of a man whom he respected entirely and held in no small degree of affection driving himself up a blind and damaging alley from which only shock tactics could free him. Soon after that, McCoy wrote an open letter to the *Racing Post* to apologise for upsetting people at the meeting, and said: 'Think yourselves lucky – I have to live with me all the time.' If it is true that sorry is the hardest word, I don't suppose it comes easy to the hardest man in the sport.

To an extent, the memories of bad times suggest that McCoy is a tortured soul, but he isn't. He is just driven in a way that nobody other than someone who has ridden countless jumps winners will ever truly understand.

He is hugely liked in the weighing room, and it is notable that he is one of the only people not wearing a skirt who makes John Francome's face light up when he walks in the room, partly because Francome thinks he is a remarkable jockey but mainly because he plain likes and values the man.

At 34, McCoy just wants to go on doing what he has done more successfully than anyone else. He says: 'You don't think about the dangers and I have always convinced myself that I will get up again. I would never want to train as I just wouldn't have the patience, not least with the owners.'

What fires McCoy up is the things to come. He has an excellent relationship with JP McManus, another intensely private individual, and says: 'I can go out for an evening and talk to him about anything. He is another power for good around the place, and I am very happy that things have been going so well at Jonjo's with the horses holding on to their form so well.'

He describes himself as 'hopelessly soft' when it comes to 15-month-old daughter Eve, and says: 'I spoil her rotten, but she is the only person who always smiles every time I walk into the room – it has never happened before with anyone else!'

McCoy trots out phrases such as 'You get spoilt by being on good horses' or 'I am lucky never to fall below a high threshold of fitness' and 'I have been fortunate to have good doctors' as if any one of

'It's usually much wetter than this at Plumpton, Tiger.' McCoy and Woods at the JP McManus charity pro-am in County Limerick.

'In an age of tin gods and idle idols, there is something about this savagely competitive man that sets him apart and places him alongside the tiniest handful of genuinely special sportsmen.'

ALASTAIR DOWN

these things was some sort of accident. They are not, they are the direct product of his iron will.

There is something implacable and remorseless about him, and yet the human warmth is all there. He is an assiduous visitor to fellow jockeys in hospital, and tales are legion of how he will drive miles and turn up out of the blue to make a presentation or visit that will literally be life-enhancing for the recipient.

There were some very stupid people who took time to warm to McCoy both as a man and a jockey. I know, I was one of them. But every now and again, as you watch him and his lodger stoke a pair of them down to the last, you understand what is meant by the words 'golden days'.

There was a moment a couple of years ago when McCoy and Walsh both fell at the same fence in the Arkle Chase on fancied horses. As they hauled themselves to their feet, the rage, frustration, fury, ambition and dented pride radiated off them and generated enough power to heat a town. Then they were off, trudging back to the stands for the next round, partly mad the pair of them, but wholly magnificent.

Looking at the paint-spattered one-off in his kitchen, you strain for signs of the marks his life has left on him. You think of the hundreds of thousands of miles driven to gaff tracks on dire days, of slow boats and wicked jumpers being driven into open ditches or hurled at the last. You remember the wasting, the broken bones, the blood, and those darkest of days when a friend's peg in the weighing room lay fallow, never again to feel the hand of the man who left his clothes on it before going out to do his job of work.

And as you drive away, it is hard not to feel a surge of gratitude for the sheer good fortune that your time has coincided with his. In an age of tin gods and idle idols, there is something about this savagely competitive man that sets him apart and places him alongside the tiniest handful of genuinely special sportsmen.

Raise a glass to him. In fact, make a night of it – and raise it 3,000 times or more.

*That piece was published the day after the 2,998th winner was
landed on a horse called Stradbrook, by a nose in a three-way blanket
finish at a rain-sodden Stratford-upon-Avon. But any thoughts that
it may have only just been written in time were scotched as blizzards
and rain and ordinary racing misfortunes kept McCoy winnerless and
the historians record-shy for a full ten days longer.*

*Then in truly terrible weather at Plumpton the winners finally
came, though not without the fates first delivering a dramatic final-
fence crash just to remind us that they are ever present.*

David Baxter reported.

TONY McCOY finally reached his personal landmark of 3,000
career jumps winners with success aboard Restless D'Artaix in the
2m1f beginners' chase at Plumpton on Monday.

Just half an hour after being cruelly robbed of victory when Miss
Sarenne fell at the last with the race seemingly in the bag, McCoy
returned to the saddle and demonstrated the strength of mind and
body that has set him apart and seen him land the jockeys' title an
unprecedented 13 times.

He sat just behind the front-running The Package throughout,
and then moved to dispute the lead turning into the home straight.
Timmy Murphy didn't give up easily on his mount and the pair
jumped the last two fences together, but McCoy was not to be denied
again and drove the seven-year-old out to the line to create history.

McCoy said afterwards: 'It's not something I'm going to play
down – I am ecstatic.

'All 3,000 winners have taken a lot of hard work.

'It's very easy to be driven when you are lucky enough to do a job
you love.

'I am lucky to have been supported by a number of great people
over the years.'

McCoy was also quick to pay tribute to his agent after his
landmark success: 'It's great, I've been very lucky with my agent.
A lot of thanks must go to Dave Roberts. He's helped me since I
started and, without him, this wouldn't be possible.'

Earlier in the afternoon, winner 2,999 had been achieved courtesy of Hello Moscow, which had seen the champion at his brilliant best, cajoling the horse from over a circuit out to a neck victory.

Nicky Henderson provided McCoy with three of his four rides and, after sharing the agony of Miss Sarenne's fall, was quick to praise the legendary rider.

He said: 'Just as you see it today, it couldn't be wetter, it couldn't be colder and he can ride winners like that and finish like that – it's quite extraordinary. I think he is the only person who would have won on either of them.

'You'll never see numbers like that again. I cannot ever see him stopping because that's the way he is.'

Not for the last time, the Racing Post *rolled out the tribute pages – but it was really the last time for one of the paper's most popular writers Sir Clement Freud, as sadly he was to die just two months later. Clement had been at Plumpton, and in his regular Saturday column added his own slightly cryptic take.*

I WATCHED AP McCoy at Plumpton on Monday. The going was arguably the worst on which horses have ever raced in the UK, but the track wanted a mention in the history books and they did not abandon.

The champion jockey managed the two successes that brought his tally to 3,000. Me, I think 2,998 (the number he had been sitting on for more than a week) is a terrific number of winners to ride, exactly 2,997 more than I managed during my own career of starving – thereby having near-terminal halitosis – sitting in saunas and hogging diuretics before the weigh-out. Not that there remained in me a lot of disposable liquid.

Records, as people continually tell us, are made to be broken and AP, who is only just over 1,000 wins ahead of his nearest rival, wanted to do it significantly. The fact is, achieving a round figure in wins or major golf championships or runs or

At last: 3,000 up as Restless D'Artaix wins the Tyser & Co. Beginners' Chase at Plumpton on 9 February 2009.

aces in tennis is considered important and obscures actual achievement.

Geoff Boycott, for whom I never had any affection, felt that making a century was vital, all-important, what cricket is all about. Kevin Pietersen, who would not be my choice as 'nicest man in white flannels', last week scored 97 against the Windies, which was considered by many and widely reported by hacks to have been a manifestation of failure, as if cricket hinged on centuries, half-centuries, hat-tricks and more stumpings in an innings than had previously been achieved.

In fact, cricket is about beating the other side, which you do by scoring more runs, taking more wickets and holding more catches.

Four wickets by one bowler in a single innings may not get his name inscribed on a shield in the pavilion but is entirely helpful in scuppering the opposition, as are 97 runs from the bat, though accorded a quieter yelp of joy than greets that of the centurion. Ninety-seven runs, folk tend to forget, are helpful to any batting side and are only a tear-jerk away from getting hugged by the batsman at the other end.

The winner's enclosure for the 3,000th time.

Clement's last day's racing was a successful one at Exeter, the day before he died on 15 April 2009. A month earlier he had lunched well at Cheltenham and watched McCoy give the ultimate answer to anyone who billed him as merely a numbers man.

Wichita Lineman's victory was one of those moments that could not happen but did. Three fences out no other soul bar McCoy, and certainly not the horse himself, considered winning to be a likely option. But Clement, and the rest of us, could leave wondering at what we had seen. Tony Smurthwaite filed the story.

FOR JP McMANUS, day one of the 2009 festival will go down as close to perfect thanks to two wins, including a memorable and reportedly unique 1-2-3 in the cross-country chase, and having the crowd serenade him on his 58th birthday.

McManus was as wowed as everyone else by the power of Tony McCoy for win number one. The champion jockey never gave up on the willing Wichita Lineman in the 22-runner William Hill Handicap Chase and grasped victory from the edge of defeat with a last-stride defeat of long-time leader Maljimar.

'Words can't describe his dedication to the game and his will to win,' said McManus of McCoy, 'and the other side of him, his sympathetic nature.

'As long as he kept asking the horse, the horse kept responding to his urgings.'

Winning trainer Jonjo O'Neill was equally moved, saying: 'That's what McCoy is all about. He was just magic.'

As if there were any need for re-emphasis, McCoy then signed off this 14th championship season with more of the vintage touch. Jon Lees was at Sandown Park to see the final flourish.

THERE were winners galore in another championship-winning campaign for Tony McCoy but many of the prestige prizes had gone elsewhere until on the final day of season the inimitable

Overleaf: William Hill Trophy at Cheltenham, 10 March 2009: Wichita Lineman (white blaze) in pursuit of Nenuphar Collonges (Robert Thornton) at the last.

209

McCOY'S SEASON 2008-2009	
wins:	186
rides:	853
strike rate:	22%
position in championship:	1st

jockey produced one of his vintage efforts to snatch Bet365 Gold Cup glory on Hennessy.

Trainer Carl Llewellyn may have given up hope, but McCoy has forged a reputation on defying probability and his perseverance was fittingly rewarded when Hennessy denied Briery Fox in the dying strides of the £165,000 race.

It was heart-stopping for Llewellyn and owner Malcolm Denmark and heartbreaking for connections of Briery Fox and luckless rider Mark Bradburne, who had thought victory was theirs as they jumped to the front at the last fence.

Hennessy was back in fourth place with six lengths to make up but, in a performance reminiscent of McCoy's Cheltenham success on Wichita Lineman, he swept past his three rivals up the Sandown hill to win by a short head with Lacdoudal third and long-time leader Church Island fourth.

Llewellyn, godfather to McCoy's daughter Eve, said: 'He was good, wasn't he? At the Pond I thought he had a chance, but the rest of the race I didn't think he had much chance because he was never really flowing, not jumping that well. He didn't jump the Railway fences that well but it was just my luck we had the right guy on top.

'It was a hell of a ride. He was beat at all stages. Going to the first I was happy and after that I wasn't, until two circuits later. He's a tough horse and he's not very quick, but he keeps going. AP is amazing. The rest of us could win on horses that were the best horses but he consistently wins on horses that aren't the best horses, which is the true test.' Wichita Lineman was McCoy's only Cheltenham festival win this season, while his other significant victories were in December when he took the Lexus Chase on Exotic Dancer, Boylesports Hurdle on Binocular and Tingle Creek on Master Minded.

He rode Hennessy after agent Dave Roberts had picked him out as one 'open to improvement.'

McCoy, who was winning the race for the second time, said: 'I wanted to make the running and he was okay for a bit, but then he

Bet365 Gold Cup at Sandown Park, 25 April 2009: Hennessy and AP (checked colours) before the heat is turned on.

was off the bridle because we went too quick. He has a tendency to jump left and that was making him get into the bottom of a few because he was getting rushed, but I still thought at the Pond fence if I got to the bottom of this lad he'd keep going.

'Every jockey that goes out there is determined to win a race like that. You need a willing horse that is going to get you in that position but when you get on a lazy horse like that you have to find a happy medium.' Briery Fox will go down as a gallant loser, though connections were cursing McCoy. 'I used to quite like that fellow McCoy,' said trainer Henry Daly. 'I thought coming to the last that we'd got the race won, but as soon as they jumped the last I saw McCoy and thought "Bollocks!"'

McCoy had now dominated for the whole of the first decade of the new millennium. When Steve Dennis went to interview him in December 2009, he found someone prepared to talk like he had never talked before.

THERE are two Tony McCoys.

There's the one we see, the most successful jump jockey in history, a legend in his own lifetime. Then there's the one he sees, the one for whom every success is never quite enough, the joy generated from it barely sufficient to span the gap to the next success.

How else do you explain a man who has dominated his sport like no other, possessing 14 consecutive championships, 3,186 winners, the unalloyed respect of every professional and the cupboard love of every hungry punter, uttering the words, 'I'm not saying that I've ever been at the top.'

On his occupation

'If it always felt like a job, I'm not sure I'd want to do it.

'Of all my achievements, to break Sir Gordon Richards' record for winners in a season is by far my greatest. I rode 289 winners in 2001-02 and I put that way above everything else. To ride that many winners in a season you need so much luck. It was bigger than getting to 3,000 winners. When I hit 2,000 I thought I should be able to get to 3,000. Can I get to 4,000?

'Apparently I told the *Daily Telegraph* I wouldn't be riding when I was 40. I hope I didn't say that, I could ride when I'm 40.

'I still feel the same as I did ten years ago, I still love riding, I still enjoy it, it still has the same effect on me whether it be good or bad. Good days have a good effect and bad days have a bad effect, and I can't cope any better with the bad days than I could ten years ago.

'I'm better at publicly disguising it, better at going through the motions. I got worn out with people telling me I looked grumpy, so it's better that I just put on a fake smile, pretend I'm really happy.

'I wish I'd done that a lot earlier, I would have come across as a nicer person. Not that it bothers me how I come across. I probably am as grumpy as everyone thinks, but it would have looked better.'

On the Grand National

'Yes, the Grand National, there's no point in talking about it, is there,' he says, but he's smiling. 'It just hasn't happened. From a public perspective the National is the biggest horserace in the world, and so from that point of view I'd like to win the National. It will be disappointing if I don't ever win a National.'

Clan Royal was going strongly when he was baulked to a standstill at Becher's second time round in 2005, but that's not the one that claws at McCoy's contemplative moments. Four years earlier, the race had fallen apart like a cheap suit and McCoy thought his chance had come.

'Blowing Wind was the worst, much worse than Clan Royal. When the loose horse carried Blowing Wind out ... oh ... so many had got wiped out at the Canal Turn, the reins had gone over Beau's head, there were only three or four of us left.

'I thought Blowing Wind had really taken to the race. I think on that day he'd probably have won a National. But I'll have another go and see what happens. I'll have four or five more goes ... six or seven ... ten goes,' and he's laughing now.

'I'll still be trying to win it when I'm 45.'

On small meetings

'Obviously I want to go to the big meetings on a Saturday, but do I really want to go to Cheltenham and smile at everyone and then follow all the lads around and go home without a winner?

'I didn't want to go to Lingfield, but Nicky Henderson had one in the novice chase that looked as though it would win if it got round, and I had a few other fancied rides. I certainly didn't want to go to Cheltenham for the rides I could have had there.

'I don't begrudge Ruby [Walsh] and Paul [Carberry] their success ... [and then he grins wickedly] ... obviously I begrudge Ruby and Paul. But I wouldn't swap the championship for winning a Gold Cup, not a chance.

'We've all got different goals. I've won the Gold Cup and I do want to win it again. But ever since I was champion for the first few

> 'It will be disappointing if I don't ever win a National.'

TONY McCOY

215

times I've wanted to leave an impact on racing, and when I look back and ask myself, "Could I have ridden any more winners?", I'll be able to say no, I couldn't.

'As much as I want to win those big races and beat Ruby and Paul, I'm a realist. My goal is still to ride 200 winners a season, and there's still a good chance of that this year.'

On the move from Pipe

'I don't have any regrets. JP McManus asked me to ride his horses,' he says. 'It was a new challenge, something different. JP was always a man I admired and our ambitions and interests in racing were the same. I'd been champion jockey, and the challenge was to see if I could be champion without Martin's backing.

'No matter what anyone thinks, Martin totally changed the art of training a racehorse. Paul Nicholls will probably be the most successful jump trainer ever but Pipe had more impact, and he'll probably never get the credit he deserves because he's not everyone's cup of tea. I was very privileged to ride for him as long as I did, to learn what I learned from him.

'I told Martin that I'd been approached, told him that I would ride for JP because I fancied the challenge, and I cried in his house because I was leaving him, it had that much of an effect on me. It wasn't an easy decision, but it was something that was right for me at the time and I'm glad I did it.'

On the championship decided by prize money not winners

'I'm probably not the right one to ask about it. I'd have missed out on five or six championships if the title was decided that way, and if that was the case you'd probably find yourself taking a different approach to riding. If you were lucky enough to ride for Paul Nicholls, or Aidan O'Brien on the Flat, you could probably just ride at weekends. But we can't all ride for them.'

Would you he bother going to certain meetings, say, Ludlow on a Monday? '[Long pause] … I'd probably still go because I like going riding, you know. I'm probably one of the stupid ones who'd still go!'

On Sports Personality of the Year

'I didn't become a jockey to get accolades. I became a jockey because I love racing and I love riding, and that's what does it for me. I wanted to be good at what I did, I wanted to be successful, but I didn't want people to pat me on the back and say, "Well done." This may come across wrong, but I'm totally self-centred in my own little world of what makes me happy. Winning makes me happy, and I don't need someone else to tell me "Well done." People reading this might think I'm an obnoxious prick for saying that – but that's what makes me happy. I'm proud of the recognition I've received, of my MBE, for example, but for me it's not about that. Anyway, as for Sports Personality, I was delighted that Ryan Giggs won it, even though he's a Man Utd player. I think he's the greatest footballer ever in the Premier League, the complete professional. And that's me talking as an Arsenal fan.'

On falls

'I used to say I was unbreakable, but obviously I'm not. I've got enough metal in me to prove otherwise. I still think I'm unbreakable, though. The first thing I think about when I hit the floor is how long I'm going to be off. When you're lying on the ground, you just know.

'I'll know when I feel I'm not being as successful as I should be.'

TONY McCOY

'Everyone calls the fall I had from Arnold Layne at Warwick in January last year a terrible one, but that one just finished me off from a bad fall I'd had at Lingfield six weeks earlier. I got kicked hard, and I didn't sleep for six weeks.

'I kept riding, of course. I thought it was going to get better. It would have got better. But I knew when I hit the floor off Arnold Layne that I wasn't going to get up. I wasn't able to get up. I physically couldn't move.

'I convinced myself for years that I'm a fast healer, but I don't actually know whether I am. Mentally it helps, though. You can convince yourself it's not so bad.'

On death in the afternoon
'When Gloria Victis got killed in the Gold Cup I was in pieces afterwards. I didn't ride afterwards. I couldn't.

'He was an amazingly talented horse. When he won the Feltham, to this day I don't think I've had the same feel from another horse, he could jump and go so fast.

'A couple of years later I thought Valiramix was a good thing, but he fell and broke his shoulder. The Champion Hurdle was only the third race of the meeting and I didn't handle it very well. I couldn't cope with it, I couldn't cope with the idea of the horse I thought could be a superstar being killed. Gloria Victis was probably handled as badly, but it wasn't the second day of the Festival the day after.

'Ten years after Gloria Victis, I'm probably able to deal with that kind of thing better. I know that if you need to sulk or grieve you're better off doing it away from the public eye, keeping it away from everyone else. But you become a jockey because you love horses, they're the reason you do it, and death still has an effect. When Wichita Lineman was killed, I just cried. But, to put it in perspective, in the time I've been riding there've been human tragedies too.'

On giving up
'I'll know when I feel I'm not being as successful as I should be. That will make my mind up. I don't think there's anything worse

than a sportsperson who's been very successful carrying on too long at what they do.

'I wouldn't keep riding if I wasn't champion. How can you be champion jockey for 14 years and still think you're successful when you're not champion?

'When it happens, it'll be cut and dried, no period of indecision. I've always had that fear, fear of people saying he's not what he was, he should have packed up 18 months ago. I'm not saying that I've ever been at the top, mind …

'Would I change anything about the last ten years? I wouldn't mind being 25 instead of 35, that's the only thing I'd change. I wouldn't mind having another go at it.'

On favourite horses

'Black Jack Ketchum was a cool little horse. It was just a shame he had lots of problems after his novice year. He was a great character, really likeable. He wasn't overly big but had the look of a real dude of a horse. You knew when you looked at him that he was smiling back at you – and he was hugely talented. Brave Inca was a favourite of mine, and believe it or not Deano's Beeno was a favourite too. People always said that I used to beat him but I actually really liked the horse, he was a character. I became a fan of Butler's Cabin, because he won an Irish National for me and was a big winner for JP and Jonjo. And I'm still a fan of Binocular, even after he was beaten at Newcastle. There are horses I actually like riding for reasons other than they have a chance. They might not be the best horse in the world, but I like riding them for whatever stupid reason it is. They do something for me.'

By this stage you would not imagine any reasonable fan would cast doubts on McCoy's horsemanship. Well you should, because the absolute rule in racing is that one defeat, or in particular one fall, will leave some to start muttering lines like 'Well, he may be a great jockey, but I am not sure he really suits this …'

It happened to AP in February 2010. When Ruby Walsh opted to ride 2007 and 2009 Gold Cup winner Kauto Star rather than

'He was a character': AP with Deano's Beeno.

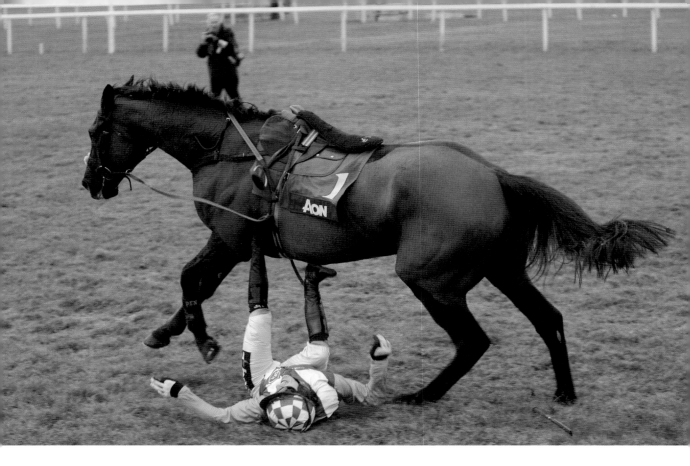

Parting company: AP and Denman in the Aon Chase at Newbury, 13 February 2010.

stablemate and 2008 winner Denman at Cheltenham that March, McCoy was the obvious choice for the ride on the other part of what promised to be the ultimate Cheltenham showdown.

But first the warm-up at Newbury. As Bruce Jackson reported, it didn't go to plan, and it was a good job Paul Nicholls was made of solid stuff.

THE glorious uncertainty of racing was never better illustrated than in the five minutes it took Denman and new partner Tony McCoy to go from heroes to zeroes under an intense spotlight in the Aon Chase.

Nobody could foresee their fate as Denman, winner of the last running of this Grade 2 race before his Gold Cup win of 2008, warmed to the champion after a couple of fences and bounded round, only to slam into the fourth last, losing a length's lead, and then land atop the next to get rid of the champion.

Denman's joint-owner Harry Findlay summed up the feeling when saying: 'It's a real shock. I thought he was jumping great for

Tony and never jumped better. I gave him nine out of ten for his jumping until the fourth last.

'I haven't talked to Tony yet but I thought he was still no offers to win the race before the mistake. He's still clear second favourite in my book, and as far as I am concerned Tony rides him at Cheltenham.'

As the fallout continued, a different picture was painted by both McCoy, who had taken a long look round off the home turn, and Nicholls.

McCoy said: 'I was disappointed when I looked round and hadn't shaken off Niche Market. I asked him and never felt him lengthen. When I got into him I thought he would attack the fourth-last, but I didn't get any acceleration and he got into the fence, and then he landed in the middle of the third last.

'I'm disappointed for Paul Nicholls, Harry Findlay and Paul Barber because they let me ride him when a lot of people think I shouldn't be riding him. Hopefully, I will get another chance in the Gold Cup; we will see.

'This happens in racing and I can only try to do my best.'

Jessica Lamb was able to report how AP's fortunes had improved within the hour.

DITCHED by Denman, triumphant in the Totesport Trophy – 40 minutes in the life of Tony McCoy.

The disappointment of defeat on 'The Tank' in the Aon Chase would have been enough to knock some jockeys off the ball, but McCoy dusted himself off and drove Get Me Out Of Here through the field – and the final hurdle – to deny Ronaldo Des Mottes, Manyriverstocross and 11-2 favourite Mamlook.

McCoy's joy meant the bad luck transferred on to Trophy kings Gary Moore and Nicky Henderson as Moore's Harry Tricker fell at the fourth, ending any hopes of a fairytale race hat-trick, while Henderson's Spirit River left his hind legs in the third last, scuppering any hope of a place, never mind victory.

Newbury, 13 February 2010: Get Me Out Of Here recovers from an unorthodox jump at the last hurdle to win the Totesport Trophy.

Shortly after Barry Geraghty and Spirit River had faded, the Seven Barrows second string Stravinsky Dance followed suit, which meant that Henderson would not snatch the race for the fifth time in the last eleven runnings.

Instead, from the penultimate flight, the £150,000 contest was set for David Pipe's Pond House or Jonjo O'Neill's Jackdaws Castle, but McCoy was a man on a mission.

'He's a fair little horse and it's a nice race to win,' said O'Neill. 'He's always been a grand lepper – it was just inexperience at the last.'

The turning treadmill of a champion's season means that there is always another challenge just a step away. So working towards Denman's Cheltenham date with destiny included an Imperial Cup win at Sandown on Qaspal carrying just 10st 3lb, the lightest that McCoy had drawn since May 2007.

Three days later Binocular, the Champion Hurdle hope of whom McCoy and most of his supporters had long despaired, came brilliantly right on the first day of the Festival.

IT WASN'T a new approach but Binocular completed one of the most unorthodox preparations for Cheltenham when transformed from Champion Hurdle non-runner to Champion Hurdle winner yesterday.

Ruled out of the race last month with an apparent muscular problem only to be ruled back in last week after being given a clean bill of health, JP McManus's six-year-old rediscovered the form that had been so absent from his other performances this season to claim the crown his connections long believed him capable of obtaining.

What exactly had been troubling Binocular during defeats at Newcastle and Kempton and an unconvincing victory at Sandown remains unclear, but the horse Tony McCoy believed would win three championships, even after last year's third placing, claimed his first with a clear-cut victory from Khyber Kim in the Smurfit Kappa-sponsored race.

Trainer Nicky Henderson's second successive victory in the race, which he captured a year ago with Punjabi, and fifth win in all, puts him alongside Peter Easterby as the most successful trainer in the race's history, yet it would not have happened if connections had scratched the horse from the race, as they were invited to do after initially announcing he would not run at Cheltenham.

Recounting developments that were reminiscent of when New Approach won the Derby – after trainer Jim Bolger had declared he had no plans to run at Epsom – and led to Binocular being laid at 999-1 on Betfair, Henderson said: 'This wasn't a ploy, I can assure you. We'd talked with AP and JP. John Halley, JP's vet, thought there was a problem. He thought it would be better to discontinue, then when we found nothing on the scans we could see no harm in returning to training. At one stage we thought it might be prudent to put him away and that is why we said that.

'We were trying to keep everyone informed. That was our opinion at the time. We did our best to keep the public informed. There were only two ways to do it, not being honest or being honest. I was being honest. With exchanges at the moment there

has only got to be one rumour that he is going for a scan and all hell breaks loose.

'Having decided that we weren't going to run, Weatherbys or the BHA rang me to ask me to scratch the horse. I mentioned it to JP and agreed with him that while he is still in we have the option to change our minds. That was probably quite a good decision.'

During the uncertainty, Binocular spent ten days in Ireland, where he underwent a bone scan before returning to Lambourn with the tests revealing no problem yet no reason for his poor jumping displays that sparked the investigations in the first place. But he continued having treatment.

Henderson added: 'Mary Bromiley was treating the back of his neck, John Halley was treating a hind leg, Buffy Shirley-Beavan was treating the sacroiliac. With a lot of work from a lot of people it has paid off somehow. It was actually difficult to say what made the difference, but the difference was big.'

That was evident as Binocular jumped fluently to cruise on to the quarters of the pace-setting Celestial Halo at the second-last. From there he sped into a clear lead to score by three and a half lengths, with stablemate Zaynar in third.

A windfall may have landed on McManus, who admitted to having 'a few pounds on him prior to him running at Sandown' when the horse was cut to 6-1 from 8s.

'To be honest, I could have torn up my ticket, but luckily I didn't,' he said. 'I felt a lot of anticipation last year. Only a week ago Nicky said I think we have a shout and he worked the oracle. Champions are hard to come by and he is a champion.'

McCoy was sufficiently elated to admit: 'I am not as miserable as you think, am I? It's hard to win at the festival. I don't think I've had such a torrid time as everybody else thinks, but this is everything.

'For some bizarre reason I just had no feel for Binocular all season. At Sandown I had written in my mind there was no way I can win the Champion Hurdle performing like that, but on

Opposite: Cheltenham, 16 March 2010: Binocular sprints up the hill to land the 2010 Smurfit Kappa Champion Hurdle from Khyber Kim ... and earn a grateful hug from his jockey.

Wednesday morning [when he schooled] I couldn't give any reason why he shouldn't be running.

'I don't know why he came alive today but he did, thankfully.'

Binocular made things look so easy that there was an almost ecstatic look about McCoy as he returned to the winner's circle. But at Cheltenham, more than anywhere, ecstasy always holds the door ajar for agony. Two days later it did that and then asked him back in again. Even a seasoned watcher like Graham Dench couldn't hide his amazement.

WE ALL know there's no tougher man in our small world than Tony McCoy, but you may be hard pressed to name a tougher sportsman on the planet.

Barely an hour after a crushing first-fence novice chase fall, McCoy was back in the Cheltenham winner's enclosure, his chin stitched and his neck aching but a Grade 1 winner yet again on old ally Albertas Run, the bold front-running winner of the Ryanair Chase.

Asked how he was, he played down the pain and replied: 'It's nothing. I've had three or four stitches in my chin and I got kicked in the head and the back of the neck. I'm sore, but I'm not dead.'

McCoy gave his former RSA Chase winner an inspired ride, soon pushing the pace along with fellow front-runner Deep Purple and asserting before the home turn. Albertas Run was a couple of lengths clear and so missed the trouble when favourite Poquelin and the mare J'y Vole had a coming together, but he would have won anyway and stormed up the hill four and a half lengths clear of Poquelin and J'y Vole, who were separated by just a nose.

The following day Denman's reputation was restored when McCoy rode him to a highly honourable second place behind Imperial Commander in the Gold Cup, and the day after that AP donned the JP silks again for the Midlands Grand National.

Opposite: Ryanair Chase, Cheltenham, 18 March 2010: Albertas Run leads Poquelin and J'y Vole at the second last.

Compiling this book is to digest such an overdose of amazement that there are times when you go back on the unblinking data of the Racing Post *website just to check that the facts were as we have said they were.*

One of those occasions was Synchronised winning the four-mile 24-fence Uttoxeter showpiece. Was it really ground so heavy that only three horses finished and AP had to dismount from his exhausted partner after the line to get him back to unsaddle? Had the horse really looked so reluctant over the first few fences that we thought he would not complete one circuit, let alone three? Did it still look as if he would get beat on the run-in?

David Carr's report shows that the memory was true.

YOU don't keep AP McCoy down for long. Two bone-crunching falls at Cheltenham and the blow of a Gold Cup near-miss on Denman might have had a mere mortal lying low. But not the champion.

He bounced back with another outstanding ride to capture the John Smith's Midlands Grand National on Synchronised, showing once again his uncanny knack of turning apparently certain defeat into big-race victory in the £80,000 feature.

His mount, a late withdrawal from the National Hunt Chase at Cheltenham, was taken off his feet early on, so much so that McCoy had to give the 15-2 shot a reminder before they had even jumped the first fence and again after the fourth.

But 4m1f is a long way on heavy ground and McCoy persevered, getting JP McManus's seven-year-old into contention on the final circuit. He joined front-running L'Aventure at the second-last fence and though the former Welsh National winner rallied, Synchronised landed the prize by three-quarters of a length.

The pair came a distance – calculated by our race-reader Walter Glynn as 104 lengths – clear of Giles Cross, who was the only other of 17 runners to complete the course.

Reflecting on the early part of the race, McCoy said: 'I wanted to take my time but I was dropping him in and he just wouldn't go. I gave

Synchronised (AP) pips L'Aventure (Daryl Jacob) to land the John Smith's Midlands Grand National at Uttoxeter, 20 March 2010.

him a smack and then I sat up on him and I got him into the bridle. I knew off the pace I was going if I could keep him alive and keep him in touch I would have a squeak in the second half of the race.

'It was a good training performance. He was in at Cheltenham but Jonjo thought the ground might not be soft enough for him and thought he would have a big chance here.'

Jonjo O'Neill said: 'The jockey didn't do too bad and the horse did fantastic!'

So once again to Aintree. Dared we dare to hope that this, AP's 15th Grand National year, might be different? Funnily enough, the vibes for the National were so moderate, particularly from AP himself, that Friday's celebrations seemed likely to be as good as it would get.

WHATEVER it is that preys on Gold Cup winners at Aintree clearly doesn't apply to Albertas Run, as he followed up his Ryanair Chase triumph with victory in the John Smith's Melling Chase yesterday.

An unexpected winner at Cheltenham, his odds of 8-1 at Aintree suggested he still had something to prove to the betting public, but under a dynamic ride from Tony McCoy he was more than up to the task as he repelled Forpadydeplasterer and Monet's Garden to take the Grade 1 prize for Trevor Hemmings.

'It's always a worry coming on from Cheltenham when running in Grade 1 races that are close together, but there were no other real fresh horses in there except Monet's Garden, who ran well,' said McCoy.

'Since he dropped back in trip I've ridden him more aggressively and he's shown a lot of pace, which he didn't do before.'

McCoy said Albertas Run was a much more confident horse on good ground and they were the only pairing that could live with the bold-leaping Monet's Garden, eventually taking the grey's measure from four out.

Kalahari King fell at the second, Schindlers Hunt sadly fractured a leg in a fall at the third and was put down, and Poquelin, the Ryanair runner-up, was struggling when unseating Ruby Walsh four out.

Winning trainer Jonjo O'Neill said: 'He's just come right this spring and is in great form with himself.

'He missed one down the back straight but otherwise everything went great and, although Forpadydeplasterer was cruising when they jumped the second-last together, I thought he would keep going and the others would have to pull out all the stops.

'It never really entered my head to worry that he'd been to Cheltenham as well, because he was in great order. AP knows him so well, they are a brilliant combination.'

The extraordinary thing about Don't Push It's Grand National triumph is that beforehand, for very good reasons, most serious racing people did not fancy him. You may remember that the horse had first come into our consciousness and these pages when he was the winning end of an horrific McCoy week which started with his teeth being smashed at Cheltenham and included more falls and an overnight collapse and hospital trip to Swindon in 2005. Four and a half years on Don't Push It had last been seen hopelessly tailed off in a hurdle race at Cheltenham only three weeks before.

But public money backed him down to favorite in the dream of a McCoy National. Not many of us shared that dream, and the jockey himself had taken an age even to opt to ride the horse. But if Don't

Push It and his jockey went out with low hopes, they came back to sky-high fulfilment. Jon Lees recorded this greatest of Grand National moments.

TONY McCOY has been racing's champion during 14 record-breaking years, but yesterday he became the public's champion when he clinched the one success he craved more than any other.

There were two other men who had endured a long and fruitless pursuit of the John Smith's Grand National in owner JP McManus and trainer Jonjo O'Neill, but it was McCoy to whom it mattered most when Don't Push It carried him past the Aintree winning post at the 15th attempt.

John Smith's Grand National, 10 April 2010: Don't Push It and AP (white cap) in the thick of it.

When his previous efforts to win the prize have been thwarted,
notably when Clan Royal was carried out by a loose horse when
leading five years ago, McCoy has cut a frustrated and dejected figure,
one resigned to being known as the best jockey never to win the
National.

Yet yesterday, having had little expectation that Don't Push
It would end the sequence, he shed tears as the barren run was
halted in front of 70,341 racegoers. McCoy, accused in the past of
being too driven and not smiling enough, admitted to being 'a big
wuss' as he dissolved at having overcome his greatest challenge.

He said: 'It means everything to me to win the Grand
National. I've won lots of big races and I'm supposed to be a

Second Becher's: Don't Push it follows Hello Bud (spots) and Big Fella Thanks.

good jockey, but to not win the National would be a bit of a negative on the cv.

'Everyone knows about the National, so from a public point of view to win the biggest race in the world means everything. At least I can feel now that I've done all right.'

McCoy's wife Chanelle added: 'This means the world to him. It's a very emotional day for a man who doesn't get too emotional.'

McCoy owed his victory to McManus, who had four runners in the field, and particularly O'Neill, who had persuaded the jockey to pick Don't Push It over stablemate Can't Buy Time.

In truth McCoy had not rated any of the mounts available to him, but once yesterday's race got under way, after an initial false start,

Overleaf: On the run-in, the grinning can begin as Don't Push It goes clear of Black Apalachi.

it was not long before he would be forced to revise that judgement.

Settling in the main body of the field, he bided his time as Conna Castle set a brisk pace. He held that advantage until well into the second circuit when persistent pursuer Black Apalachi moved ahead at Becher's Brook.

Denis O'Regan was travelling well on the Dessie Hughes-trained challenger, and with six fences to jump there were only a handful still in with a serious chance. Ominously for O'Regan, one of them was McCoy on Don't Push It.

O'Regan poured on the pressure and had the measure of Big Fella Thanks and Hello Bud – who was giving 17-year-old amateur Sam Twiston-Davies a dream debut in the race – going to the last, but Don't Push It would not relent and McCoy had his day, driving his mount past on the run-in to win by five lengths. State Of Play came from well back to claim third.

McCoy said: 'I felt after a mile this horse could win the National. I am aware how long it is in the straight. You are always worried about going too early, but every time I pulled him out and gave him a little bit of light, he picked up a little bit. He did run pretty well over 3m3f in November with a big weight and I had it in the back of my mind that he would stay.

'My trainer put me on the right one. I couldn't have picked it. He was very adamant and I couldn't argue with him.

'The one thing this horse has is ability. A few years ago Denman beat him in a novice chase at Cheltenham. He fell twice at the downhill fence at Cheltenham in the Arkle and he fell in a handicap a year later, but he seemed to like what he was doing.'

Reminded that Mick Fitzgerald had described winning the race as 'better than sex', McCoy replied: 'He's got married again since! No comment. Ask someone else that question.'

McManus had had 33 runners in the race before yesterday and one of this year's quartet was ruled out at the very start when King Johns Castle refused to race.

'AP has it on his cv and so have Jonjo and I, so we killed three birds with one stone,' he said. 'It's just a very, very special day for

us all. AP really deserved to win this race and I'm just so glad it was on one of mine.'

O'Neill never got further than the Canal Turn in seven attempts as a jockey and had had 15 failures since turning to training.

'Everybody wants to win the National,' he said. 'You think it's not going to happen. You are disappointed to get beat, but there is only

one thing you do. It's nice to complete what you want to do and it's great for AP.'

Don't Push It is a 20-1 shot to repeat his success next year, while McCoy is 10-1 with Coral to win BBC Sports Personality of the Year. He failed to make the shortlist last year but, asked about his prospects this time, retorted: 'I don't know what that is!'

Lee Mottershead had exactly the right words.

ABSOLUTELY marvellous. Rarely has racing been blessed with a better day than this. No matter how many Aintrees, Cheltenhams or Epsoms we experience, no matter where in the world the sport grabs our attention, no matter who, no matter where, no matter when.

Thanks to Tony McCoy, to whom racing owes so much, we now know that as good as it gets is so very good indeed.

His greatness is well and rightly documented. Yet until now, despite more than 3,000 winners, 14 jockeys' championships and countless major victories, he had been unable to burst from within the bubble that confined him to our lives and not the ones lived by everyone else. Only by winning the Grand National, the one and only race that really matters, was the magnificence of McCoy ever going to be appreciated by the wider world. Now, at the 15th time of asking, it has happened and, glad to report, it feels every bit as thrilling as we hoped it would.

On passing the post, he was like a changed man. Almost immediately, there were tears and no attempt to hide them. 'I'm being a bit of a wuss, but it means everything to win the Grand National,' he said, his words, his emotions, his display of sheer euphoria showing just how much it did mean. It meant more than anything he had ever achieved.

And yet, he evidently thought there was little chance of it happening. For weeks, we had asked, as we always ask, which horse McCoy would ride in the National.

There was the strongly fancied Arbor Supreme, the former second King Johns Castle, Can't Buy Time and Don't Push It. At one

AP'S GRAND NATIONALS		
year	*horse*	*finishing position*
1995	Chatam	fell 12th
1996	Deep Bramble	pulled up 28th
1998	Challenger Du Luc	fell 1st
1999	Eudipe	fell 22nd
2000	Dark Stranger	unseated 3rd
2001	Blowing Wind	3rd
2002	Blowing Wind	3rd
2003	Iris Bleu	pulled up 16th
2004	Jurancon II	fell 4th
2005	Clan Royal	carried out 22nd
2006	Clan Royal	3rd
2007	L'Ami	10th
2008	Butler's Cabin	fell 22nd
2009	Butler's Cabin	7th
2010	Don't Push It	WON

From racing's household names …

'It was absolutely brilliant. I rode in the first at Lingfield and then rushed back to watch the race with the kids.

'I thought Tony gave the horse a fantastic ride and I felt just as emotional as he did. I nearly shed a tear with him, but I managed to speak to him about an hour later. He was delighted and I was delighted for him.

'Tony has definitely got it all now, and he deserves it. It was also great for JP McManus and Jonjo O'Neill; they are all legends of jump racing.

'I know how Tony feels because I had to wait 15 years to win the Derby, although I guess the National is a bit harder to win than the Derby.'

FRANKIE DETTORI

'It was the most exhilarating day for all of us, and it was fantastic to be able to welcome Tony in his rightful place at the end of the National.'

SIR PETER O'SULLEVAN

stage, rumour had it that Arbor Supreme was favoured, only for McCoy to silence the whispers by claiming Can't Buy Time was his likely mount, although all the talk was irrelevant.

'None of them have a chance,' he told one reporter earlier in the week. But one of them had to be his, and once the decision was made, McCoy, as is his wont, convinced himself that he could win. In the minutes leading up to the race, it seems everyone else became convinced as well.

You only had to watch the betting to see what punters think of McCoy. Don't Push It should have been a 40-1 chance, yet he opened on course at 20-1 and, in an unstoppable, frenetic, scarcely believable chain of events, ended up 10-1 joint-favourite.

McCoy made it happen, not because of anything he said, but because of what his legion of fans know he can do. On a horse he described as 'mentally unstable', he did it, giving Don't Push It the perfect National ride, so perfect that he could afford himself a long glance towards runner-up Black Apalachi after the last, at which McCoy fearlessly fired his willing mount.

It was then that triumph was assured, but not until the post was passed would Jonjo O'Neill or JP McManus have begun celebrating. For them, as for McCoy, the Grand National has been a long and painful experience, and it is to them, as much as to McCoy, that credit is due. Such is AP's domination of the sport that it is he who will hog the headlines, but he could not have done it without them.

'It's a great result for racing and I'm over the moon for AP.

'I was gutted picking myself off the floor after The Package went at the 19th, but when I was walking back and looked up at the big screen and saw who was winning the race it brought a big smile to my face and made me happy.'
GRAHAM LEE

'It's brilliant for AP and for JP. They both deserve it as they give so much to the game and it's great to see them getting something big like the National, having tried to win the race for so long.'
BARRY GERAGHTY

'It's great for AP and great for racing. He probably had enough money anyway and doesn't need the prize money! But I'm thrilled for him for lots of reasons, including the fact that I lived with him for about a year and a half when I was based in England some years ago.'
DAVID CASEY

Both JP and Jonjo have, in cancer, fought a tougher foe than a handicap chase at Aintree. Now they have done the double. O'Neill, as decent a man as you could find, has finally conquered a race that had battered him as trainer and jockey. McManus, although bolstered by many millions in the bank, is, when it comes to horses, endearingly soft, supporting a vast string, many of whom are blessed with just a modicum of talent. It doesn't seem to bother him. The bills are always paid.

But it is McCoy who made this the day that it was. His joy was our joy. To a man, from his comrades in the weighing room to his followers in the grandstands, betting shops and living rooms, his crowning moment will have been received with delight. This was a groundswell of good feeling the like of which we have not previously savoured.

Now, at long last, let him be handed the recognition he deserves. Give him his due, give him the BBC Sports Personality of the Year award – heck, give him the keys to Downing Street if he wants them. Tony McCoy has won the Grand National. What a joy that is to write.

Triple first: Jonjo, JP and AP.

The Racing Post *received hundreds of letters praising McCoy and his Grand National achievement. Each one added to the chorus of praise, but these are two with special resonance.*

EVERYONE at Alder Hey Children's Hospital would like to send huge congratulations to AP McCoy.

It was a truly emotional day as we watched our much-loved Imagine Appeal Patron achieve his dream.

With the loyal support he has given to the hospital over many years, he has always been an inspirational figure of courage and determination.

For him also to think of us at the moment he won by donating his leading rider of the meeting award was overwhelming – but so typical of the thoughtful, kind AP we know and love at Alder Hey.

We are so very proud to have his support and we simply could not be happier for him, Chanelle and Eve.

JAYNE HAUXWELL
Alder Hey Children's Hospital, Liverpool

BRITAIN'S JOCKEYS would like to pay their own tribute to champion jump jockey Tony McCoy on his achievement in winning the Grand National for the first time.

AP has rewritten the record books during his career in the saddle, but a singular omission in his own mind was a victory in the Grand National.

No-one watching the aftermath of the race could have failed to have been moved by how much the win meant to him. It wasn't just those who had backed Don't Push It who were happy with the result – everyone recognised the sense of personal achievement for one of racing's greatest-ever jockeys.

AP is a wonderful ambassador for our sport and we are lucky to have him. Hopefully, we can now look forward to him making the shortlist for the 2010 BBC Sports Personality of the Year – then the

whole nation would get a chance to show their appreciation of his talents and achievements as a sportsman.

On behalf of all your colleagues and the Professional Jockeys' Association team: 'Well done, Champ.'

KEVIN DARLEY
Chief executive, Professional Jockeys' Association

The reaction had been deep and nationwide. It had been intensely moving to be there, to be down on the track as he stood up and roared at the glory of it all. It seemed to me something way beyond all that had gone before.

This is how it felt to me that Sunday.

DON'T ever underestimate what happened on Saturday. As McCoy looked up at the stands and pumped his fists high in triumph he sealed a pact not just between himself and his sport, but between that sport and the nation. For now the world could truly see the diamond we have at the very heart of things.

The crowd sensed it too. The roars that echoed around Aintree had a unique sound – not just of salute but of recognition. In 40 years of reporting at Aintree and much further afield I have never heard the like of it – not at Twickenham or Wembley, not when Ballesteros walked up the 18th at St Andrews, nor even when Usain Bolt trotted round the stadium that first incredible night in Beijing. For in none of those other places was there quite such a sense of how much of a life had been on the line.

True, Frankie Dettori was also on his 15th attempt when he won the Derby on Authorized and, at 36, was actually a year older than AP was on Saturday. But for all Frankie's popularity and his 'to-hell-and-back' plane crash experience, there was not really the feeling that winning the Derby meant absolutely everything to him. With McCoy there was a nakedness about it. For 15 astonishing, unbroken championship years he has become a byword for wanting to win in every race every day. Now we could see how he had wanted this one more than all the rest.

Again he stood in his stirrups and punched the air, again the cheers thundered down and with them the remembrance of all he has put himself through to ride those 3,000 winners, and more especially all that has happened on this most public of stages. Seven times he has hit the floor in his National attempts, and almost every one of the thousands in the stands and the tens of millions watching around the globe will have glimpsed the most famous drama when the loose horse wiped him out on Clan Royal right on the brink of take-off at Becher's five years ago.

The Grand National is the one time racing invites the world in, and it has been able to share our fascination that McCoy, the most implacable, self-flagellating competitor in any sport, could also be a decent and surprisingly funny human being.

As the tributes flooded in, outsiders could see what we have known for some time – that his opponents don't just admire AP as a practitioner, they like him as a man.

When he came through for the press conference the most hardened of hacks stood to cheer. For we know, too, that McCoy does not play cheap shots. Whenever he can be, he is helpful. He is an example not just to racing but to sport itself. How important do you have to be not to answer a sensible question? How tough not to be able to be generous to your fellow players? How grand to not let little defeats also matter?

As he talked there was an extraordinary sense of fulfilment in his voice. Of how this was the one race that involved everyone, of how proud it would make everyone who had helped him along the way, of how it may even one day get through to his Ruby-worshipping daughter Eve. But there was something more than this one race, even those soon-to-be 15 championships, about his satisfaction. In the last month, he had won two and been second in the third of the three greatest jump races. He was speaking from the very top of his personal mountain and the view was great.

Yet the very wonder brings the worry with it. Because you have to ask not how much higher, but for how long? For not even McCoy's remarkable physique and indomitable will can last into his 40s, and so the shadows of his career were lengthening in that Aintree sun. He is far too positive to allow that to pass his lips – did you see him on that hurdler at Southwell yesterday? But part of the public reaction was because they recognised those shadows too.

Which leaves them one last challenge. Last Wednesday, a small but very special group gathered in Yarmouth, Isle of Wight, to salute the 80th birthday of the rugby and wider sporting legend that is Cliff Morgan. Among those present were Henry Cooper and Mary Peters, winners of the BBC Sports Personality of the Year in 1967, 1970 and 1972.

They both won their awards not just for what they did, but for what they were. When we talked of the Grand National, they both asked about McCoy. They did not say it, but they know, we know, and the world should know, that he belongs among their number.

For what happened on Saturday should be celebrated not just by racing but by the whole sporting world.

The morning after the day before: Don't Push It and AP at Jackdaws Castle.

It is now not only us who can be proud of him.

For all of us, even for McCoy himself, the Grand National triumph had seemed a sticking point. But if you are a champion of champions you do not stick for long, nor fail to let reality in.

So on Thursday 22 April, AP was delivering another big winner in the green and gold McManus colours when Captain Cee Bee picked off his field in Punchestown's featured Ryanair Novice Chase. And two days later, on finale afternoon at Sandown, he was reflecting on yet another table-topping season.

TONY McCOY, speaking yesterday on becoming champion jockey for the 15th consecutive time, revealed that he had harboured doubts about his chances of winning the title again.

Although McCoy finished 34 winners clear of his nearest pursuer Richard Johnson, a slow start to the season (by his standards) left the Grand National-winning jockey feeling vulnerable about his ability to retain his prize.

McCoy, who also collected the Channel 4 Racing People's Jumps Season Award, said: 'Up until Christmas I didn't think it was going to happen, as I hadn't had a lot of luck.

'The last six weeks to two months have been amazing, though. What every jockey dreams about is winning the Grand National – it really is a dream come true.'

McCoy was handed his award by former England rugby union star Brian Moore, who reflected the obvious opinions of the appreciative crowd in saying that he was 'humbled to be in the presence' of the champion.

As well as his Aintree victory, McCoy also picked out Binocular's win in the Smurfit Kappa Champion Hurdle as a highlight.

'I couldn't believe that Binocular got beat the year before,' McCoy said. 'This season started badly for him but I always believed he could win the Champion Hurdle.'

It was, however, his win on Don't Push It in the National that made him the happiest in another successful year.

McCoy added: 'It was amazing. All the emotion at Aintree with 70,000 people there – it was something I could only dream of. You only get one chance a year and people don't know how much luck you need.

'Better jockeys than me haven't won the Grand National, so before the race I said to myself I was in great company, but to win the race – it really was something I'd dreamed about.'

The close of the Grand National-winning season and an incredible 15th consecutive championship seemed an appropriate time to close this book. But six weeks later, in early June 2010, the Queen intervened and gave Alastair Down the chance to sum up in regal style.

BETWEEN a visit to the Derby and a busy five days at Royal Ascot next week the Queen yesterday awarded Tony McCoy an OBE in her Birthday Honours list. In the 58 years of her reign she will not have made a more thumpingly popular decision as far as racing fans are concerned. Spot on, Ma'am.

AP's OBE is for 'services to horseracing' and none has given of himself so unsparingly and unstintingly as the man whose pre-eminence has now racked up an extraordinary 15 champion jockey titles in a row. It amounts to official recognition of what jumps fans have known for the best part of twenty years – that our time has been made special by a sporting phenomenon the like of whom has never been seen before.

Most people would run up the white flag faced with just a single working day of AP's life – the hot-bath sweats, the ferocious amounts of energy expended and the ever-present risks run.

As a young man, there looked to be times when AP himself found the grind too unforgiving, too savage to sustain. But if ever a man grew with the telling of his tale, became greater with the forging of his own legend, it is McCoy.

The pounds shed, the starship mileage racked up in the quest to be the best, the hundreds of falls and the injuries, both serious and superficial, which have been shrugged off are just a part of the man.

McCOY'S SEASON 2009-2010	
wins:	195
rides:	874
strike rate:	22%
position in championship:	1st

And celebrations continue . . .

Throughout everything, in times good and bad, there has never been so much as a moment when he has done anything other than try his heart out.

It was seeing all those years of unflagging effort gain the greatest reward of all that made AP's Grand National victory such an imperishably precious occasion. That heartwarming and climactic triumph of a lifetime spent in the drive position seemed to kick open the last locked door to his soul. AP had always ached to win the National but not until that indelible moment did we realise how red-hot that ambition burned and just how much it was needed to make his career complete.

There was on that Aintree afternoon the palpable feeling that in some very profound way justice had been done. And gloriously so.

Part of the joy in watching McCoy has been to see the wracked and almost haunted figure of years ago find, through family life, satisfactions and levels of contentment that he probably thought were for other people.

It is no surprise that McCoy is revered in the jumps weighing room, as in that sanctuary he is surrounded by those who understand his brilliance best. But through his sheer longevity and the unremitting way he goes about his work it is with the racing public that he has forged a unique bond.

And we don't stand to applaud him for his technique or even the unprecedented winning tallies he has racked up. What has caught our imagination and made AP memorable is his character. It is the man himself.

I can think of nobody else in racing who enjoys such universal trust. And that is because he has never let either himself – or the public – down. Yesterday he was awarded an honour, but in truth it is an honour for all of us to have him about the place.

AP McCOY: THE CAREER IN SUMMARY

FULL NAME Anthony Peter McCoy

BORN Ballymena, County Antrim, 4 May 1974

PARENTS Peadar and Claire McCoy

APPRENTICESHIP Billy Rock 1987-89, Jim Bolger 1989-94, Toby Balding 1994-95

FIRST RIDE IN A RACE Nordic Touch on Flat at Phoenix Park, 1 September 1990 (finished seventh)

FIRST WINNER Legal Steps on Flat at Thurles, 26 March 1992

FIRST RIDE OVER JUMPS Riszard, brought down over hurdles at Leopardstown, 17 March 1994

FIRST WINNER OVER JUMPS Riszard, over hurdles at Gowran Park, 20 April 1994

FIRST RIDE OVER FENCES No Sir Rom, fell at Galway, 30 July 1994

FIRST RIDE IN BRITAIN Arctic Life, runner-up over hurdles at Stratford, 13 August 1994

FIRST WINNER IN BRITAIN Chickabiddy over hurdles at Exeter, 7 September 1994

FIRST WINNER OVER FENCES Bonus Boy at Newton Abbot, 4 October 1994

FIRST GRAND NATIONAL RIDE Chatam, 1995 (fell 12th fence)

1,000TH WIN OVER JUMPS IN BRITAIN Majadou at Cheltenham, 11 December 1999

3,000TH CAREER WIN (Britain and abroad, jumps and Flat combined) Kilbeggan Blade, Towcester, 18 January 2009

3,000TH WIN OVER JUMPS IN BRITAIN AND IRELAND Restless D'Artaix at Plumpton, 9 February 2009

MOST WINS IN A BRITISH SEASON 289 in 2001-02 (beat Gordon Richards' previous record of 269 on Flat in 1947)

CHAMPION CONDITIONAL RIDER 1994-95 (with a record 74 winners)

CHAMPION JUMP JOCKEY every season since 1995-96, up to and including 2009-10

CHELTENHAM GOLD CUP WINNER Mr Mulligan 1997

CHAMPION HURDLE WINNERS Make A Stand 1997, Brave Inca 2006, Binocular 2010

QUEEN MOTHER CHAMPION CHASE WINNER Edredon Bleu 2000

GRAND NATIONAL WINNER Don't Push It 2010

KING GEORGE VI CHASE WINNER Best Mate 2002

McCOY'S SEASONS 1994-95 TO 2009-10
OVER JUMPS IN GREAT BRITAIN

	wins	runs	%	2nd	3rd	4th	win prize	total prize	£1 stake	runner-up (wins)
1994-95	74	469	16%	63	56	50	£222,568	£361,746	-14.28	
1995-96	175	759	23%	131	89	71	£736,087	£1,005,678	+ 90.63	D Bridgwater (132)
1996-97	190	666	29%	130	78	52	£1,016,413	£1,279,787	+1.21	J Osborne (131)
1997-98	253	831	30%	163	93	69	£1,183,334	£1,681,628	- 20.62	R Johnson (120)
1998-99	186	768	24%	115	85	71	£900,577	£1,262,395	- 134.91	R Johnson (133)
1999-00	245	803	31%	136	91	58	£1,329,379	£1,737,964	+10.46	R Johnson (142)
2000-01	191	775	25%	131	82	73	£916,502	£1,435,893	-122.74	R Johnson (162)
2001-02	289	1006	29%	185	132	85	£1,958,944	£2,755,657	-74.61	R Johnson (132)
2002-03	258	840	31%	131	118	60	£1,918,826	£2,606,213	-31.55	R Johnson (147)
2003-04	209	800	26%	144	111	54	£1,401,768	£2,032,216	-131.24	R Johnson (186)
2004-05	200	821	24%	143	92	74	£1,443,632	£2,072,318	- 48.80	T Murphy (142)
2005-06	178	828	21%	125	99	79	£1,688,700	£2,429,370	-137.57	R Johnson (167)
2006-07	184	758	24%	117	97	67	£1,539,965	£2,272,807	-122.15	R Johnson (154)
2007-08	140	648	22%	99	80	45	£959,978	£1,574,029	-129.95	R Johnson (122)
2008-09	186	853	22%	136	101	72	£1,511,714	£2,302,676	- 78.29	R Johnson (132)
2009-10	195	874	22%	140	96	84	£2,131,384	£2,950,022	-138.67	R Johnson (161)
	3153	12,499	25%	2089	1,500	1,064	£20,859,771	£29,760,399	- 1,083.08	

In addition, in seasons 1994-95 to 2009-10 inclusive, AP had 94 winners
over jumps in Ireland from 584 rides. And he rode six winners from 69 rides
on the Flat in Ireland between 1990 and 1994.

INDEX

254